GROWING & DISPLAYING
ORCHIDS
A STEP-BY-STEP GUIDE

GROWING & DISPLAYING
ORCHIDS
A STEP-BY-STEP GUIDE

Authors
Wilma Rittershausen • Gill & David Oakey
Photographer
Neil Sutherland

SMITHMARK

CLB 3139
© 1993 Colour Library Books Ltd., Godalming, Surrey
Printed and bound in Singapore by
Tien Wah Press (PTE.) Ltd.

ISBN 0-8317-5182-7

10 9 8 7 6 5 4 3 2

This edition published in 1994 by SMITHMARK
Publishers Inc., 16 East 32nd Street, New York,
NY 10016.

SMITHMARK books are available for bulk purchase for
sales promotion and premium use. For details write or call
the manager of special sales, SMITHMARK Publishers Inc.,
16 East 32nd Street, New York, NY 10016;
(212) 532-6600

Credits
Edited and designed: Ideas into Print
Photographs: Neil Sutherland
Typesetting: Ideas into Print and Bureau 2000
Production Director: Gerald Hughes
Production: Ruth Arthur, Sally Connolly,
Andrew Whitelaw, Neil Randles

Half-title page: The superb *Miltoniopsis* Flamboyant.
Title page: *Phalaenopsis* Pink Chief x Fairvale and Pink
Chief x Zuma Cupid combine to make a dazzling display.
Copyright page: *Phalaenopsis* Babette - a spotted variety.

CONTENTS

Part One

GROWING ORCHIDS

Orchids have been popular in cultivation for nearly 200 years, ever since the first exotic specimens arrived in Europe from the newly explored tropical and subtropical regions. They are one of the most successful plant families and grow on every landmass, from the equator to the very edge of the Arctic Circle. In the tropical zones they have reached their zenith, with flamboyant blooms of incredible richness and variety. These are the epiphytes, or air plants, that grow on trees but are not parasitic. Most of the epiphytes produce swollen stems known as pseudobulbs that hold reserves of water for the plant and also support the leaves and roots. Roots are often exposed to absorb moisture from the air. In the cooler, temperate zones, orchids grow in the ground as terrestrials, producing rosettes of leaves and blooms from the center.

Orchid plants may be sympodial, meaning that each season they produce either independent flowering growths or pseudobulbs from a horizontal rhizome. Cymbidiums, for example, produce pseudobulbs, while paphiopedilums produce growths. Others have a monopodial system and produce a vertical rhizome from which new leaves grow from the center. Vandas, for example, have long rhizomes and phalaenopsis have short ones. Orchid blooms are unique and incredibly diverse. All have three sepals, which resemble the petals, and three petals. One petal, called the lip, is different and is designed to attract pollinating insects. A single central structure, the column, contains the male and female parts fused together and hidden from view.

This section looks at some of the most popular orchids and how to grow them. As an introduction to their enchanted world, we hope that it will stimulate you to look more closely at these fascinating plants.

Vanda Rothschildiana, a famous old hybrid first raised in 1931.

Cymbidiums

Cymbidiums are the most widely grown orchids. Their well-deserved popularity stems from their ease of growth and the wonderful range of hybrids available in all colors, from white and cream to yellow and green, and from pink to red and bronze. Their flowering season extends from late autumn throughout the winter and spring to the late-blooming types in early summer. From a collection of mixed hybrids you can expect to have blooms for almost nine months of the year, and these blooms will last for a good eight to ten weeks. The flower spikes are usually taller than the foliage and may be upright, arching or pendent in their habit. The plants produce rounded pseudobulbs that may be the size of an egg or as large as a tennis ball. Each supports eight to ten narrow leaves, which may be 18-24in(45-60cm) long. They produce vigorous, thick and fleshy roots.

Most of the species that have been used to create the modern hybrids come from the Himalayas in India, with a few others from Burma, Vietnam, Taiwan, China and parts of Australia. These species include *Cymbidium lowianum, insigne, traceyanum, pumilum* and *devonianum*. The cymbidium species themselves are not so generally grown and are usually confined to specialist collections.

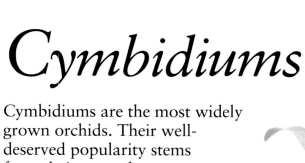

The tall spike of La Belle 'Annabelle' AM/RHS can grow up to 1m(39in) and needs plenty of headroom.

Above: *Fleshy white roots pushing through the compost indicate an active root system. A pseudobulb cut in half reveals the healthy white tissue that holds the plant's vital water reserves.*

Right: *Select your cymbidium hybrids from a range of varieties and colors, with different lip markings. If pseudobulbs shrivel, cut off the flower spikes and keep them in water to reduce the strain on the plant. Supply a nitrate-based feed to encourage strong new growth.*

Jessie 'Blakistone' is typical of the miniature varieties that are highly suitable for growing indoors.

Cooksbridge 'Pinkie' is another successful hybrid. It has attractive, delicate pastel coloring.

York 'Ever Blooming' is an older cymbidium variety, but still very popular with growers today.

The parents of this new top-quality variety are Quetivel Mill and Granos Vaux.

Basically, there are two groups of cymbidium hybrids to choose from: the miniatures and the standards. The miniature varieties have come later to prominence but excel over the standards because they are more compact, bloom more freely, are less demanding of light and carry more blooms per flower spike. This makes them better suited to growing indoors, where so many of them are now seen. Their blooms can be 2-3in(5-7.5cm) across the petals.

The standard varieties are bigger all round, with blooms up to 5in(13cm) across. Adult plants can become exceedingly large and difficult to handle, requiring pots of 12in(30cm) or more in diameter. However, a fine, well-grown plant of this size with six or more 36in(90cm) flower spikes in full bloom is quite breathtaking, and hard to beat. If you have the space and headroom in a greenhouse or sun lounge, think big!

Growing cymbidiums

Cymbidiums are cool growing, so provide them with a temperature no less than 50°F(10°C) on winter nights, rising by 10-15°F(5-8°C) during the day. Lower temperatures than this will restrict their growth and affect their flowering, as will much higher levels at night. The summer temperature should not exceed 85°F(30°C) by day. Higher temperatures will stress the plants and cause premature leaf loss, again affecting their flowering. Shade cymbidiums from direct sunshine throughout the summer and give as much light as possible during the winter. Wherever practical, grow cymbidiums outdoors in summer. Water plants all year round, and feed in spring, summer and autumn. Spray the leaves daily in summer.

Below: Cymbidium madidum *is an unusual variety from Australia.*

Cymbidium madidum has been used successfully to produce some delightful yellow hybrids.

GROWING CYMBIDIUMS

Seasonal activity
Plants grow nearly all year. Flowering period winter to early summer. Evergreen.

Location
Greenhouse or conservatory in winter. Keep outside in summer if possible. Miniatures will grow indoors.

Temperature
Summer maximum: 85°F(30°C)
Winter day: 60-65°F(16-18°C)
Night minimum: 50°F(10°C)

Light/Shade
Shade from direct sunshine in summer, provide maximum light in winter.

Watering/Spraying
Water all year round. Spray leaves daily in summer.

Feeding
Spring, summer and autumn.

Right: This example of the hybridizer's art shows the Indian species Cymbidium devonianum (left) with one of its hybrids, Sea Jade 'Freshwater' AM/RHS.

Both C. madidum and C. devonianum produce pendent flower spikes, a reminder that these epiphytic orchids grow on trees in the wild.

Odontoglossums & Miltoniopsis

Any of the orchids within this group are ideal for the beginner and make good subjects for growing indoors, in a conservatory or in a greenhouse. What is more, they include the most gaily colored flowers of all the orchids. Odontoglossum blooms are uniquely patterned, with individual designs to a degree that no other orchid has achieved. Their pseudobulbs are oval, from light to dark green, with four narrowly oval leaves, the center pair being 6-9in(15-23cm) long. They have an abundance of fine roots. Miltoniopsis are similar, but carry five leaves, their paler coloring matching that of the pseudobulbs. Only a few of the species within these groups are available to growers due to their scarcity. The hybrids offer a far wider range of colors, as well as being more robust and therefore easier to grow. Much interbreeding with additional, closely allied genera within this group, including *Cochlioda*, *Oncidium* and *Brassia*, has produced the intergeneric hybrids that have given rise to the fantastic variety now available. The most popular genera are *Odontioda (Odontoglossum x Cochlioda)*, *Odontonia (Odontoglossum x Miltoniopsis)*, *Odontocidium (Odontoglossum x Oncidium)*, *Vuylstekeara (Miltoniopsis x Odontioda)* and *Wilsonara (Odontioda x Oncidium)*. Further man-made genera within this group become considerably complex and all are loosely referred to as odontoglossum types. These hybrids can be traced back to the original South American species, most of which come from high elevations in the Andes. Their range extends from Mexico, through Colombia, crossing the equator to Peru.

This cutaway view of the pot reveals the healthy root system, with live roots actively progressing through the compost.

A clone of Odontioda La Hougie Bie.

Vuylstekeara Cambria 'Plush' FCC/RHS is one of the most popular varieties today. Note the large, flared lip, which has come from crossing with Miltoniopsis.

Above: A mature odontoglossum can be comfortably accommodated in a 5in(13cm) pot. This is a healthy plant, with good color to its foliage. All its pseudobulbs are in leaf. Strong new growth is developing well at the front of the plant and this will develop into the next flowering pseudobulb.

Right: This selection of modern hybrids shows odontoglossums, odontiodas and a Vuylstekeara. Selective breeding for over 100 years has created the range of colors and contributed to the variety in size and shape of blooms.

Odontioda *Marie Noel, a* top-quality variety.

Note the superb rounded shape of this fine example of Odontioda *Aloette x Flocalo.*

The species Odontoglossum crispum *has been involved in the breeding of all the plants shown on this page.*

The rich color of Odontioda *Marie Noel originated from the red* Cochlioda noezliana.

Odontioda *La Hougie Bie is a lovely yellow hybrid.*

Odontoglossum *Augres extends the variation in color combinations.*

Because of their involved breeding, these hybrids do not have specific flowering times. Mostly, they bloom as their latest pseudobulb nears completion at the end of the growing cycle. Vuylstekearas will regularly bloom approximately every nine months. The miltoniopsis, being less interbred, will have their main flowering in early summer, with a secondary display in the autumn. However, the quality of the blooms may not be of the same standard on the second flowering, or when they bloom in the heat of the summer. They should last in perfection for up to six weeks.

Left: Two young plants of identical age. The one on the left is flowering, delaying the start of the new growth. On the right, new growth is well advanced. Miltoniopsis do not normally grow and flower at the same time.

Right: A group of very colorful hybrids featuring the predominant colors in this genus. Their main flowering season is early summer and they have the added bonus of fragrant blooms.

This new hybrid is a cross between Woodlands 'Alba' and Charlesworthii, two very old plants.

Growing odontoglossums and miltoniopsis

Keep these orchids out of the direct sun and well shaded during the summer. An advantage of indoor growing is less temperature fluctuation, but avoid overheating in the summer. If temperatures exceed 80°F(27°F) for long periods during the day, either find a cooler place indoors - such as a window that does not receive sunlight - or move odontoglossums outside for the summer months. Miltoniopsis leaves are too soft for these orchids to be summered out of doors. If odontoglossums and miltoniopsis are subjected to very high temperatures, the stress can cause premature loss of leaves and possibly roots, as well as checking growth. The winter night temperatures should be no lower than 54°F(12°C).

Odontoglossum types and miltoniopsis can be watered throughout the year, always keeping the plants moist enough to maintain plump pseudobulbs. These will quickly shrivel if allowed to become overdry. At the same time, be sure to give them plenty of fresh air. Feeding can be all year round, giving less in winter, more in summer. Spray odontoglossums lightly in summer, but keep the leaves of miltoniopsis plants dry.

GROWING ODONTOGLOSSUMS AND MILTONIOPSIS

Seasonal activity
Plants grow nearly all year. Flowering period varies according to type. Evergreen.

Location
Indoors, greenhouse or conservatory. Odontoglossums can be kept outside in summer.

Temperature
Summer maximum: 80°F(27°C)
Winter day: 60-65°F(16-18°C)
Night minimum: 54°F(12°C)

Light/Shade
Shade from direct sunshine in summer.

Watering/Spraying
Water all year round. Keep plants moist. Spray odontoglossums lightly in summer, but keep miltoniopsis leaves dry.

Feeding
All year, more in summer, less in winter.

This very fine hybrid is a top variety produced in France and called Anjou 'St. Patrick'.

The darkest red is captured in the rich tones of the German-bred Hamburg 'The King'.

This is a lovely hybrid raised in the USA, called Rouge 'California Plum'.

This is 'Arctic Moon', one of the forms of the Colombian species, Miltoniopsis vexillaria, which produced these hybrids.

Phalaenopsis

The popularity of phalaenopsis has increased in recent years as they are easy to grow and bloom indoors, and can produce flowers all year round. An average plant will carry three to five 6in(15cm) leaves at any time. These are roundly oval, thick and fleshy and often glossy. New leaves grow from a central rhizome, without pseudobulbs. Among the orchids they are noted for their very beautiful roots, which often grow outside the pot, adhering to any surface that they touch. They are silvery-gray and flattened, with delicate pink or green growing tips. Always take care not to snap these off.

As with so many of the orchids, the species are in the domain of the true collector, but a multitude of hybrids have been raised for the hobby grower and these are sufficient to satisfy the most ardent enthusiast. The main species are inhabitants of the Philippine Islands and Borneo, while others are found from Thailand to Malaysia. From the species *Phalaenopsis sanderiana*, *stuartiana* and *schilleriana* have come a host of lovely hybrids in varying shades of white and pink. With the introduction of other species, including *amboinense* and *sumatrana*, many beautiful yellow varieties have been developed. To these basic colors can be added the striped and spotted types, giving even more choice.

With phalaenopsis, flower spikes follow the growth of a new leaf and it is not unusual for more than one spike to be in bloom at any one time. Sometimes a succession of

The flower spike comes from near the base, usually following the formation of a leaf.

It is quite usual for phalaenopsis to produce their roots outside the pot. These roots are alive but inactive until green tips appear.

Above: *Phalaenopsis are monopodial orchids that grow new leaves from the tip of a vertical rhizome. An average plant has three to five leaves at any time.*

When large enough, phalaenopsis will often produce a branching flower spike, as seen here on this beautiful hybrid, Michael Davis.

This semi-alba variety is one of the top hybrids raised in France. It is called Plaisir de Valec.

Left: Although their colors are limited, there is abundant variety in phalaenopsis. The plants like to be kept warm and usually do very well indoors. Their flowering season is all through the year.

These huge, rosy pink flowers are typical of another French hybrid, known as Touraine.

Spotted varieties are very attractive, as is clear from this latest variety, which is called Babette.

Barbara Moler x Misty Green, produced along different breeding lines, is smaller in stature.

bloom is produced, extending the flowering period even further. In addition, cutting back a flower spike to a lower node will almost always create a second blooming on that spike. In this way, it is possible for a single mature plant to be in bloom for nine months at a time.

The blooms can measure up to 4in(10cm) across, the generous petals spread wide and flat, partially concealing the sepals. The lip is small and neat, either delicately marked or flushed a deeper shade.

Growing phalaenopsis

Phalaenopsis will adapt remarkably well to indoor culture, provided they are kept in a warm spot away from drafts and out of direct sunlight. In a greenhouse or conservatory, where they will mix happily with other orchids, they also require good humidity to balance a high temperature of 65°F(18°C) at night, rising by 20°F(12°C) during the day, and the normal variation between summer and winter temperatures. The plants will not die if grown at temperatures lower than those recommended, but they will not flourish so well and may be susceptible to leaf or center growth rot. A leaf can collapse and become 'watery' overnight. Indoors, you can sponge or lightly mist their leaves every day to keep them fresh and free from dust. Confine greenhouse spraying to the summer months and never make it so heavy that water runs into the center of the plants.

Water phalaenopsis all year round, keeping them evenly moist without overwatering. Encourage the growth of any roots that are overhanging the pot by spraying them. Remember that once growing in the open, the roots cannot be put back into the pot. Phalaenopsis grow all year round, albeit at a slower pace during the winter, and so you can feed them lightly all year, decreasing the frequency during the dullest winter months. Underwatering will cause dehydration and the leaves will become limp. Indoors, always keep the plants in a humidity tray with a little water just below them. In this way, they will always be near to some moisture.

Left: Phalaenopsis *Golden Emperor 'Sweet'* represents the development of the smaller-flowered hybrid. There is little difference in the size of the plant, but the flower spikes are less tall and the blooms more open and of a slightly heavier texture. Yellow is the dominant color in this very attractive group of orchids, which have been bred from Malayan species.

Right: Chamonix is typical of the large-flowered hybrids bred for many generations to obtain a perfectly round flower. Mature plants are capable of producing more flower per plant for their size than any other orchid. Sprays of a dozen or more blooms are not uncommon. These basically pink or white varieties are raised from Philippine species.

GROWING PHALAENOPSIS

Seasonal activity
Plants grow and flower all year round. Evergreen.

Location
Indoors, greenhouse or conservatory. Keep away from drafts.

Temperature
Summer maximum: 85°F(30°C)
Winter day: 75°F(24°C)
Night minimum: 65°F(18°C)

Light/Shade
Keep in shade.

Watering/Spraying
Water all year. Keep plants evenly moist. Spray exposed roots and spray plants lightly in summer.

Feeding
All year, less in winter.

Cattleyas & Vandas

These two groups contain some of the most colorful and flamboyant orchids. Indeed, their blooms are among the largest of the cultivated types.

The cattleyas make strong, robust plants with vigorous club-shaped pseudobulbs supporting one or two thickly textured leaves. These are broadly or narrowly oval, measuring up to about 6in(15cm) long. The plants have a thickened rhizome - often visible on the surface - from which the pseudobulbs grow at short, regular intervals. They produce thick, extensive roots, which can grow to a considerable length.

Because of extensive interbreeding between the related genera *Sophronitis, Laelia, Cattleya, Brassavola* and others, there are many hybrid genera in the group. These include *Sophrocattleya, Brassocattleya, Laeliocattleya* and other combinations, all of which are loosely termed cattleyas. Their flowering periods are spring or autumn, with blooms lasting up to three weeks. Nearly all are fragrant to a greater or lesser degree. The species from which the modern hybrids have been produced are epiphytic plants mainly from Central and South America. A few species are still in cultivation compared with hundreds of hybrids.

Depending upon the type created by this hybridizing, the blooms may be as small as 2.5in(5cm) in the miniature varieties, to 6in(15cm) across in the standards. Colors range from pristine white, through delicate pink, purple and yellow shades to vibrant reds, oranges and even bronze. Their magnificent lips are mostly flared, frilled and richly colored in brighter hues. The buds - maybe one or two or up to six or eight - grow from the top of the pseudobulb, usually protected in their early development by a sheath, which splits as the buds emerge.

Below: Sophrolaeliocattleya *Jewel Box 'Scheherazade' AM/RHS shows off its brilliant red coloring. This superb color, together with its compact size, has come from the species* Sophronitis coccinea.

Left: Laeliocattleya *Barbara Belle 'Apricot'* is a good example of the most popular type of cattleya. The large, decorative blooms are among the most flamboyant of orchids. Greenhouse or conservatory culture in good light suits them best.

Below: Sophrolaeliocattleya *Rocket Burst 'Deep Enamel'* shows considerable influence from the species Cattleya aurantiaca, *as well as the miniature* Sophronitis coccinea. *It bears small, bright orange blooms with an exceptionally small lip.*

Below: Another small-growing group of cattleyas is represented by this Cattleya *Miva Glossa. These cattleyas are seen in delicate pastel shades, as well as in the elusive green - a color derived from C. bicolor.*

The vandas and their close allies, the ascocendas, (*Vanda* x *Ascocentrum*) complement the *Cattleya* groups very well and the two can be successfully grown together. The vandas are tall-growing plants that produce pairs of narrow, oval leaves from a central growing point of a vertical rhizome. Aerial roots adorn the lower portion of the rhizome, which has become devoid of foliage. The flower spikes, each usually carrying six or eight blooms, arise from the base of the leaves, mainly during the summer, and last for several weeks. Although the variety in vandas is not so great, hybrids are available in superbly rich colors, including blue, red, orange and yellow. More often these colors are enhanced by interlacing lines or tessellation (also known as marbling) on the dominant lower sepals, which are flat and rounded, dwarfing the more diminutive lip.

A small number of species, mostly from Burma, have produced the hybrids of today. The most notable of these is *Vanda coerulea*, a beautiful species with sky blue flowers. When this was crossed with *Vanda (Eulanthe) sanderiana* from the Philippines, the result was one of the most famous orchids of all time - the deep blue *Vanda* Rothschildiana, which is still the best type to grow. It readily blooms two or three times a year, a performance that most other vandas find hard to emulate. Curiously, the blooms open quite pale. The color intensifies over the first few days as the flowers mature.

GROWING CATTLEYAS

Seasonal activity
Plants grow in spring and summer. They flower in spring or autumn and rest in winter. Evergreen.

Location
Greenhouse or conservatory. Miniature hybrids grow indoors.

Temperature
Summer maximum: 85°F(30°C)
Winter day: 65°F(18°C)
Night minimum: 55°F(13°C)

Light/Shade
Provide plenty of light but avoid direct sun.

Watering/Spraying
Water well in summer, very little in winter. Spray lightly in summer.

Feeding
Spring to autumn.

Growing cattleyas and vandas

Cattleyas are intermediate orchids, requiring a minimum winter night temperature of 55°F(13°C) and plenty of light. Because of this light requirement, the best way to grow them is in a greenhouse or conservatory. Indoors, they can take up a lot of space and be reluctant to bloom. However, the miniature hybrids are the exception and well suited to growing indoors. Most cattleyas have a resting period during the winter, or at some other season, when they require very little water.

Because of their growing habit, vandas are cultivated in open slatted baskets and suspended by string or wire near the glass in a greenhouse or conservatory, where they will receive plenty of light. In this position, they need a regular spray at least once a day. Cattleya temperatures will suit the vandas.

Below: The most popular and free-flowering of all the vandas is Vanda Rothschildiana, *one of the finest examples of a blue orchid.*

Cattleyas that produce a single leaf on each pseudobulb are described as unifoliate.

Note the extensive aerial roots on this vanda growing in an open basket.

GROWING VANDAS

Seasonal activity
Plants grow in spring, summer and autumn. Growth slows in winter. They flower in summer. Evergreen.

Location
Suspend in slatted baskets near greenhouse or conservatory glass.

Temperature
Summer maximum: 85°F(30°C)
Winter day: 65°F(18°C)
Night minimum: 55°F(13°C

Light/Shade
Provide plenty of light but avoid direct sun.

Watering/Spraying
Water and spray at least once a day.

Feeding
Spring to autumn.

Left: This group of cattleyas and a vanda give a good indication of the habits of the plants. All these specimens are mature plants that have flowered and illustrate a typical range of sizes. A selection of these two genera will provide exotic blooms during the year. The flowers will last from three to six weeks.

This cattleya has two leaves on each pseudobulb and belongs to the bifoliate group.

27

Zygopetalums, Masdevallias, Encyclias & Coelogynes

With so many orchids to choose from, the following is a limited selection of the more popular types. They are by no means the only ones available, merely a brief summary of some of the other varieties you can grow. They are suitable for beginners and can be kept small by dividing, if you do not want them to become too large.

Zygopetalums are handsome orchids with large pseudobulbs and four leaves. These are ribbed and narrowly oval, brittle and easily damaged. The flower spikes come from inside the first leaf on the partially completed pseudobulb and usually produce six to eight flowers measuring 3in(7.5cm) across, in a rich combination of dark brown sepals and petals and indigo lips. This is the basic coloring for hybrids produced from the Brazilian species *Zygopetalum mackayi*. These autumn-flowering hybrids are more robust and easier to grow in a cool, shady position indoors or in a greenhouse.

Masdevallias are another extraordinary genus from South America, with a variety of species and hybrids in all sizes, ranging from less than 2in(5cm) to 6in(15cm) high. They do not have pseudobulbs and their foliage can be tufted and grasslike, while the larger species have broader leaves. The flowers are characterized by the triangular-shaped sepals, which may have long or short tails. The petals and lip are minute and almost unseen at the center of the flower. Most have single blooms on a stem, a few have more, sometimes in succession. Species and hybrids are grown along with related genera, which include draculas and dryadellas. All like cool, airy conditions with shade and this is best achieved in a greenhouse. Keep the plants evenly moist - but not too wet - all year round.

GROWING ZYGOPETALUMS

Seasonal activity
Plants grow in spring and summer. They flower in autumn and rest in winter. Evergreen.

Location
Indoors or in a greenhouse.

Temperature
Summer maximum: 85°F(30°C)
Winter day: 60-65°F(16-18°C)
Night minimum: 50°F(10°C)

Light/Shade
Keep in shade.

Watering/Spraying
Water in spring, summer and autumn. Do not spray.

Feeding
Spring, summer and autumn.

Encyclia vitellina

Encyclia cochleata, the cockleshell orchid.

Masdevallia veitchiana x Angel Frost

Masdevallia corniculata

Masdevallia *Whiskers*

28

Left: An attractive and slightly more unusual zygopetalum, known as Helen Ku. This hybrid remains small and compact, producing a limited number of blooms on the stem.

Below: A delightful mixed group of orchids that will add interest and color, as well as fragrance, to any collection. They are all ideal subjects for growing in a confined space.

Coelogyne ochracea

Coelogyne speciosa *var.* alba

Dryadella edwallii

Maxillaria rufescens

Encyclias (from South America) and coelogynes (from India and Malaysia) are both pretty genera containing great variety. Many are petite and ideal for indoors. Most have elongated or rounded pseudobulbs and neat foliage, and bloom during the winter, spring or early summer. The flowers of *Encyclia* grow in small clusters on upright stems from the top of the pseudobulb, while coelogyne flowers more often appear from inside the new growth. Encyclias are sometimes fragrant and their main coloring is white to creamy white, with red-lined lips. Top varieties to grow are *Encyclia pentotis* and *radiata*, but there are others that are quite different and distinct. The fragrant spring-flowering *Coelogyne ochracea*, for example, is white with yellow on the lips, while the winter-flowering *C. cristata* has large white flowers with yellow on the lips. Grow these orchids in cool conditions in good light and give them less water in winter. Do not let the pseudobulbs shrivel as a result of underwatering. Some varieties grow extremely well and are ideal for beginners.

GROWING MASDEVALLIAS	GROWING ENCYCLIAS AND COELOGYNES
Seasonal activity Grow in summer. Flower mainly in summer. No rest period. Evergreen.	**Seasonal activity** Grow in spring and summer. Flower in winter, spring or early autumn. Rest in winter. Evergreen.
Location Cool airy greenhouse.	**Location** Indoors, greenhouse, conservatory.
Temperature Summer maximum: 75°F(24°C) Winter day: 62°F(17°C) Night minimum: 52°F(11°C)	**Temperature** Summer maximum: 80°F(27°C) Winter day: 60°F(16°C) Night minimum: 50°F(10°C)
Light/Shade Provide shade.	**Light/Shade** Provide good light.
Watering/Spraying Keep moist all year round. Do not spray.	**Watering/Spraying** Water less in winter. Spray in summer.
Feeding Spring, summer and autumn.	**Feeding** Spring, summer and autumn.

Maxillarias, Oncidiums & Epidendrums

Maxillarias can be particularly appealing if you like small flowers on miniature plants, although some species, such as M. *sanderiana* and *grandiflora*, are really large by comparison. The smaller species are suitable for growing indoors and will bloom freely in good light. The most rewarding species are M. *tenuifolia* from Honduras, which has yellow flowers overlaid with red spotting; the summer-flowering M. *ochroleuca* from South America, which has delightful filigree flowers - white with yellow or orange lips; and the winter-flowering M. *picta* from Brazil, with yellow flowers, barred red on the outside. All are fragrant and produce their flowers singly on the stem. There are very few hybrids in this genus.

Oncidiums from Central America are popular and colorful. While the species are becoming harder to find in nurseries, a few superb hybrids have all the glamor anyone could wish for. The plants are similar in appearance to odontoglossums, to which they are related and with which they will interbreed. The typical *Oncidium* produces a tall, slender stem that branches out at the top to produce a shower of bright yellow flowers. The sepals and petals are small, but superimposed by an enlarged lip, typically measuring 1.6in(4cm) across. For best results, grow at intermediate temperatures in good light, indoors or in a greenhouse. Other species, such as *Oncidium papilio* and *luridum* from the West Indies, are representative of the warmer-growing varieties.

Epidendrums are wonderfully varied and produce some very dramatic blooms. The plants range from the diminutive E. *polybulbon* from Trinidad, to the giant E. *ibaguense* from Mexico. The latter is a reed type with long stems that produce heads of bright red flowers. On a large plant it becomes perpetually blooming. Most grow cool to intermediate and like good light with some shade.

GROWING ONCIDIUMS	GROWING EPIDENDRUMS
Seasonal activity Plants grow in spring and summer, flower in autumn, and rest in winter. Evergreen.	**Seasonal activity** Plants grow in summer, flower in spring. Rest in winter (except miniatures).
Location Indoors, greenhouse or conservatory.	**Location** Large varieties, greenhouse or conservatory. Miniatures indoors.
Temperature Summer maximum: 85°F(30°C) Winter day: 65°F(18°C) Night minimum: 55°F(13°C)	**Temperature** Summer maximum: 85°F(30°C) Winter day: 65°F(18°C) Night minimum: 55°F(13°C)
Light/Shade Provide good light.	**Light/Shade** Most varieties need good light.
Watering/Spraying Water all year, less in winter. Spray in spring and summer.	**Watering/Spraying** Water well in summer, less in winter. Spray spring and summer.
Feeding Spring to autumn.	**Feeding** Spring to autumn.

Flower spikes will bore through the compost to emerge under the plant.

Left: Oncidium maculatum *from South America is a strong, robust plant that blooms freely in the early summer. It produces short sprays of brown and buff flowers.*

Right: Maxillaria sanderiana *is one of the giants of the genus. This plant is at its best when grown in a hanging basket to show off its pendent flowers.*

These are large flowers, 3.2in(8cm) across.

Above: *A stunning* Epidendrum falcatum *shows the pendent habit of the plant, which is growing on bark.*

GROWING MAXILLARIAS

Seasonal activity
Plants grow in summer. Flowering season varies according to type. Plants rest in winter. Evergreen.

Location
Smaller species are suitable for indoor growing, larger species in greenhouse or conservatory.

Temperature
Summer maximum: 85°F(30°C)
Winter day: 60°F(16°C)
Night minimum: 50°F(10°C)

Light/Shade
Provide plenty of light.

Watering/Spraying
Water all year, less in winter. Spray in summer.

Feeding
Spring, summer and autumn.

Paphiopedilums

Paphiopedilums produce beautiful mottled foliage without pseudobulbs and make decorative houseplants. Their distinctly handsome flowers are borne singly on mostly tall stems, and an unusual feature is a lip modified into a pouch, which has given rise to the popular name 'lady's slipper'. Hybrids are mostly grown from species found in Burma or Thailand. Other types, defined by their plain green foliage, have heavier, more rounded flowers.

These orchids like to be warm, so provide a minimum temperature of 60°F(16°C) and moist, shady conditions. They can be watered all year round. Indoor culture suits them well and they are often seen growing alongside phalaenopsis (see page 20). The mottled-leaved varieties may flower at almost any time, but mainly during spring and summer, and the blooms will last for many weeks. The plain-leaved types are mostly winter and spring-flowering. Keep plants in as small a pot as possible, often repottting into the same size pot. Avoid getting water into the center of growths.

The dorsal sepal is a dominant feature of paphiopedilums and is usually flared or spotted.

The main feature is the pouch, which is a modified lip. There is little variation in the basic shape.

The petals may be short, narrow or wide, depending on the variety. In some cases, they may be exceptionally long, horizontal or drooping.

GROWING
PAPHIOPEDILUMS

Seasonal activity
Plants grow most of the year. They flower in spring, summer or winter. There is no rest season. Evergreen.

Location
Indoors, greenhouse or conservatory.

Temperature
Summer maximum: 85°F(30°C)
Winter day: 70°F(21°C)
Night minimum: 60°F(16°C)

Light/Shade
Provide shade.

Watering/Spraying
Water all year. Do not spray.

Feeding
Spring, summer and autumn.

Left: This is a German-bred hybrid, known as Celle, which represents what is now the most popular type of paphiopedilum flower. Other types have more rounded blooms.

Right: This group shows mostly mottled-leaved varieties bred from the species, Paphiopedilum callosum and its hybrid Maudiae. They are known collectively as Maudiae types.

P. lawrenceanum *x Vintners' Treasure, a tall and elegant Maudiae type.*

Some specimens of Colorado produce flowers as large as this. All are very long-lasting.

Elsie x Maudiae has a small but richly colored flower.

Gowerianum van album *x William Matthews, another variation from similar breeding lines.*

Primcolor, a charming, small-flowered variety of different breeding. The flowers are produced in succession.

Nougatine, a green-leaved variety with heavier bloom, can be traced back to the species, P. insigne.

Primulinum *x Maudiae, an attractive small-flowered variety.*

Aladin produces an unusual pink flower on a shorter stem.

33

Dendrobiums

Dendrobiums come from many parts of the Old World, including Australia and New Guinea. The showiest and most popular are hybrids from the Indian species, *Dendrobium nobile*. They are easy to bloom and come in a multitude of colors from white and yellow, through shades of pink and red. All have decorative lips of distinctive coloring. They produce elongated pseudobulbs - known as canes - up to 18in(45cm) tall, with leaves at right angles along their length. Flowers are produced in twos or threes along the canes between the leaves.

Dendrobiums flower in the spring after resting. Grow in cool or intermediate conditions and remember that good light is essential for flowering. Water well in summer, but keep the plants dry during the winter.

With superb amethyst and white blooms, Ekapol is one of the most popular of the phalaenopsis *types*.

Below: *Varieties of the* nobile *type. These hybrids are highly decorative and bloom along the length of their canes. Also illustrated are* D. infundibulum *and a similar hybrid that bloom from the top half of their canes.*

Dendrobium infundibulum *is an extremely free-flowering species from India.*

Nobile *type dendrobiums bloom from older, leafless canes. It may take two years for one cane to flower out completely.*

Left: *Dendrobium* Dale Takiguchi *is a phalaenopsis type, with colors from white to amethyst. Flowering stems grow from the top of long pseudobulbs.*

The buds and stems of D. infundibulum *are covered with dense black hairs. It makes a decorative plant.*

Dawn Marie, an unusual, attractive hybrid, flowers from the top of the cane.

These plants can grow to a considerable height and require plenty of light. This nobile type hybrid is Ruby Blossom.

Note the variation between the flowers and the richly colored lips on this example of Ruby Blossom.

GROWING DENDROBIUMS

Seasonal activity
Plants grow in spring and summer. They flower in spring and rest in winter. Semi-deciduous in cultivation.

Location
Greenhouse or conservatory.

Temperature
Summer maximum: 85°F(30°C)
Winter day: 60°F(16°C)
Night minimum: 50°F(10°C)

Light/Shade
Provide good light.

Watering/Spraying
Water well in summer, keep dry in winter. Spray in spring and summer.

Feeding
Spring, summer and autumn.

Sao Paulo is another example of the breeding from D. nobile. It needs the same conditions.

Lycastes, Calanthes & Angraecums

Lycastes are a group of strong-growing orchids originating from South America. They are allied to anguloas and can be hybridized to produce the genus *Angulocaste*. They have large, cone-shaped pseudobulbs, with several wide, broadly oval, ribbed leaves that are soft in texture and are shed after one season. These orchids remain deciduous in winter. All have distinctive three-cornered flowers formed by the flattened sepals; the inward-held petals and lip are smaller. In spring, the many stems carry single flowers in a range of colors, from white, through pinks and yellows to greens and reds. Grow cool, in good light and do not spray the leaves. Allow plenty of room to grow while in summer leaf. They are best suited to a greenhouse or conservatory.

Calanthes can be tried in a warm greenhouse. They produce large silvery green pseudobulbs topped with broadly oval, shortlived leaves in summer. While resting, the leafless pseudobulbs produce an autumn flower spike that can grow to 24in(60cm), with a cascade of wonderfully soft blooms, each one 2in(5cm)

Below: Anguloa clowesii, *a wonderfully perfumed, summer-flowering species from Ecuador. The plant produces lush, seasonal foliage, becoming deciduous in the winter.*

The other name for this plant is the cradle orchid, which refers to the loosely hinged lip that can be rocked back and forth inside the cupped flower.

Anguloa clowesii *is popularly known as the tulip orchid.*

Left: Calanthe vestita *and its hybrids produce flowers in winter from the leafless pseudobulbs. Colors range from white, through pink and light red to deep cerise.*

GROWING LYCASTES

Seasonal activity
Plants grow in spring and summer. They flower in spring and rest in winter. Deciduous.

Location
Greenhouse or conservatory with space for summer growth.

Temperature
Summer maximum: 80°F(27°C)
Winter day: 60°F(16°C)
Night minimum: 50°F(10°C)

Light/Shade
Provide good light.

Watering/Spraying
Water in spring, summer and autumn. Do not spray leaves.

Feeding
Spring to autumn.

Above: Lycaste aromatica *is a small-flowered, highly fragrant variety. It blooms in profusion in the spring as the new growth starts.*

Above: Angraecum sesquipedale, *the magnificent Star of Bethlehem orchid, produces its ivory-white blooms in winter. The flowers have long spurs.*

long and colored white, pink or red with a contrasting lip. The blooms will last for many weeks over the winter and spring. The best plants to grow are hybrids produced from the deciduous Old World species *Calanthe vestita*. These like a minimum temperature of 65°F(18°C) at night. They have a short, fast growing season, when you should keep them well watered and fed, but in shade. Annual repotting suits them. Do this in early spring, when new growths are just showing.

Angraecums are epiphytic orchids suitable for a warm greenhouse or conservatory kept at 65°F(18°C) as a winter night minimum. They enjoy moist, shady conditions and plenty of growing space, since they can grow to 24in(60cm) or more. There is a small choice of species and hybrids, including *Angraecum sesquipedale* from Madagascar or its hybrid *A.* Veitchii. Angraecums found in cultivation are large-growing plants, with pairs of leaves on a central, upwardly growing rhizome. In winter, several large, white waxy flowers, each with a long spur, are produced on a long spike.

GROWING ANGRAECUMS

Seasonal activity
Plants grow all year; slower in winter. They flower in winter. Evergreen.

Location
Greenhouse or conservatory.

Temperature
Summer maximum: 85°F(30°C)
Winter day: 75°F(24°C)
Night minimum: 65°F(18°C)

Light/Shade
Provide shade in summer.

Watering/Spraying
Water all year, less in winter. Spray lightly in summer.

Feeding
Spring to autumn.

GROWING CALANTHES

Seasonal activity
Plants grow in spring and summer. They flower in winter and spring, and rest in winter. Deciduous.

Location
Warm greenhouse.

Temperature
Summer maximum: 85°F(30°C)
Winter day: 75°F(24°C)
Night minimum: 65°F(18°C)

Light/Shade
Shade in summer.

Watering/Spraying
Keep well watered in summer. Do not spray.

Feeding
Spring to autumn.

Pleiones & Bletillas

These two groups of orchids are mainly terrestrial, although they are sometimes found growing on outcrops of rock. Alone of all the orchids discussed in this book, they can be grown in an alpine house or frost-free cold frame. In mild climates, they can be grown out of doors as rockery plants, protected by a layer of straw or clear plastic sheeting from the winter frosts. The greatest danger they face is being eaten by mice.

The pleiones produce pseudobulbs with a single, narrowly oval leaf. When the new growth starts in spring, one large flower measuring 3in(7.5cm) across is produced from the center and each bloom lasts for ten days. After flowering, the new growth develops into a complete pseudobulb. The leaf is shed in the autumn and the plant rests, so you should cease watering it at this stage.

Species from Taiwan and parts of China are available, as are a range of their hybrids. The hybrids have increased the size and color combinations of the flowers, which can be found in white, pink-lilac to almost red-lilac, and yellow to apricot. The most widely grown is *Pleione formosana* and its white variety *formosana* var. *alba*. It is a good idea to repot these orchids every year, only partially burying the pseudobulbs. Do this in early spring, when new growths appear.

Above: Bletilla striata *is a delightful orchid for a cool windowsill or a frost-free alpine house. The small, richly colored flowers appear in the spring and last for up to three weeks.*

Left: *Another temperate, terrestrial orchid, the European species of Dactylorhiza can be planted outdoors and grown on to form colonies. Once planted, take care not to disturb them.*

Bletillas are deciduous orchids that produce underground tubers from which the new leaves grow in the spring. The stems can be quite tall - up to 9in(23cm) - with narrowly oval, delicate leaves. The slender flower spikes come from the center and carry an upright spray of up to a dozen, light amethyst-purple flowers measuring 1in(2.5cm) across. The usual species seen in cultivation today is *Bletilla striata*, a charming plant from China that goes well with pleiones and requires the same care. Another species also grown is *B. formosana*, a more robust plant with slender foliage and long sprays of creamy pink flowers. It blooms in early summer after *B. striata*.

Bletillas will grow in the same outdoor locations as pleiones or indoors on a cool windowsill out of the sun. Repot each year in the spring and water freely, with a little feeding throughout the summer. Gradually dry off when the leaves turn yellow and leave the plants dry to rest during the winter. These terrestrial orchids can be grown in a peat compost in half pots or pans. They are at their best when left in clumps.

Above: Pleione formosana *'Iris' is one of the most delicate orchid blooms. Pleiones like a cool, light aspect or can be planted outdoors. If frosts are frequent, dig plants up and store them in a cool, dry place for the winter. Plant out when new growth appears or keep in pots until after flowering.*

GROWING PLEIONES AND BLETILLAS

Seasonal activity
Plants grow in spring and summer. They flower in spring and rest in winter. Deciduous.

Location
Alpine house, cold frame or rockery if protected from frost. Cool windowsill indoors.

Temperature
Summer maximum: 65°F(18°C)
Winter day: 40°F(5°C)
Night minimum: 33-40°F(1-5°C)

Light/Shade
Provide shade in summer.

Watering/Spraying
Water freely in summer, but cease watering in autumn. Do not spray.

Feeding
Spring to autumn.

Left: Pleione formosana *'Snow White' is a very popular white variety. Pleiones grown in half pots provide a mass of bloom during the spring.*

39

Growing orchids indoors

Growing a selection of orchids indoors is undoubtedly the most straightforward and least demanding method of cultivation. Orchids will adjust to habitats not specially created for them and often grow extremely well and require the minimum of attention in a less than ideal environment. Indoors, the orchids are living with you and you spend much more time close to them, meeting their needs on a regular, even hourly basis! Try growing a small mixed collection on gravel-filled humidity trays. Net curtains at the window will protect them from the direct sun, and closing heavier curtains up against the glass on winter nights will ensure that cold does not damage nearby plants. If you prefer, you could grow a few orchids in a purpose-built growing case, which can provide a permanent home for a number of the smaller-growing varieties. The case can be automated with a small fan for air circulation and a humidity tray to help maintain some moisture around the plants. Bear in mind that orchids in pots indoors will dry out relatively quickly and will need frequent watering to keep them moist. Although spraying is not practical, sponge the leaves daily to keep them fresh and free from dust. Remember, a lone plant placed on a bright window with neither shade nor moisture and no other foliage around it is unlikely to succeed. Generally speaking, those orchids that do best indoors are those that need less light, particularly the hybrids. Try phalaenopsis and paphiopedilums in a warm room, and miltoniopsis, vuylstekearas and wilsonaras - along with other genera in the complex odontoglossum group - in cooler areas. The masdevallias will thrive in average temperatures when kept away from bright light.

Above: The basic essentials that you need for growing orchids indoors are a humidity tray filled with expanded clay pellets or gravel kept topped up with water. This will provide some moisture to rise around the plants in an otherwise dry environment.

Right: This type of arrangement can be used and improved upon to create a living display area featuring a variety of orchids growing with ferns and other foliage plants. The size and number of plants is only limited by the space you have available and the overall conditions. The plants relate to each other and provide themselves with their own growing environment.

Growing orchids in an aquarium

If you choose to grow some of the very tiny orchids, you may encounter problems due to their small stature. Small pots dry out within hours and the more immediate demands of these diminutive plants can be overlooked in a mixed collection. Ideally, miniature orchids need their own 'mini-micro' climate. A group of them in a finely controlled environment will succeed better than one or two lone plants competing alongside their larger relatives. An ideal solution is to grow and display them in a converted all-glass fish tank. Once inside their aquarium, the tiny orchids can remain permanently in position, either in the greenhouse or indoors. In a room setting, the aquarium should be pleasing to the eye and can include a lid with tube lighting to enhance the display, as well as adding warmth. To maintain an attractive arrangement indoors, you can also include orchids of a suitable size while in bloom and return them to their normal growing area after flowering. Some orchids suitable for this type of culture would include the smaller species among the *Pleurothallis* and related groups. Many of these produce attractive plants with minute flowers, often blooming over a long period. There are also miniatures among the masdevallias and dryadellas that make ideal subjects for growing within the confines of an aquarium.

1 *Your aquarium will need a moisture base to maintain the level of humidity. Fill it to a depth of about 1in(2.5cm) using expanded clay pellets, pebbles or a similar material.*

2 *Provide a background to show off the orchids and other plants in the aquarium. Cork bark has a natural appearance and you can mount small plants directly onto it.*

3 *You can incorporate a few miniature tillandsias (bromeliads) to lend variety and interest to the display. You can easily attach these to the cork bark with staples.*

4 *Try placing the orchids in various positions in the tank until they look their best. Position the taller plants at the back, with the smallest species at the front. Be creative!*

This *Miltoniopsis* can be shown off in the tank while in bloom, but is normally too large to grow here.

Indoors, a lid fitted with tube lighting is useful in winter. Keep the lid open a little to avoid condensation.

Coelogyne ochracea will eventually become too large for the tank, but can be displayed while it remains in bloom.

ORCHIDS AND OTHER PLANTS FOR DISPLAY IN AN AQUARIUM

Orchids
Pleurothallis grobyi
Pleurothallis aribuliodes
Dryadella zebrina
Dryadella edwallii
Masdevallia chontalensis
Maxillaria tenuifolia
Promeneae citrina
Epidendrum polybulbon
Epidendrum porpax
Sophronitis coccinea
Sigmatostalix radicans

Other plants
Miniature *Tillandsia* species
(Bromeliads)
Selaginella species
(Tree club moss)
Helxine soleirolii (Baby's tears)

It should be possible to water the plants without removing them from the tank.

Keep the water level in the base to just below the stones. This will create humidity.

If too much water collects from watering, siphon some off. Do not allow plants to stand in water.

5 It is a good idea to mist the interior of the aquarium regularly to keep up the level of humidity and to keep the plants fresh. A small plant sprayer is ideal for this purpose.

Growing orchids in a conservatory

The conservatory, or sun lounge, is an area designed for relaxation and there are several good reasons for growing orchids here. To begin with, the central heating system can be taken directly from the house and run at very little extra cost. Secondly, the more time you spend among the orchids the better you can care for them, quickly spotting any problems and dealing with them as they arise. And finally, because this is a place to relax in, you will ensure that your conservatory is comfortable - neither too hot nor too cold - and these conditions will also suit the orchids. Place staging around the sides of the conservatory and install a system that will hold moisture under the plants. If you have a tiled floor, any water sprayed or spilled can be left to dry naturally without causing damage. Use the central area for table and chairs, and a tall plant if there is space. Control temperatures by shading and ventilating, and install tailor-made curtains that can be lowered to keep out the direct sun and to keep in warmth on winter nights. You can grow a wide range of orchids in a conservatory, but it may not be easy to create different temperature zones, so choose either all cool varieties or intermediate and warm ones. If you have plenty of headroom, try a few large specimen plants, such as cymbidiums or *Epidendrum ibaguense.*

Left: *Provide a staging that can accommodate the orchids, with a moisture stage underneath. This purpose-built slatted staging allows the moisture from a water-soaked gravel bed to rise around the plants.*

Right: *A conservatory furnished with phalaenopsis, cattleyas, miltoniopsis and dendrobiums. The roof is shaded outside with green emulsion paint and ornamental blinds can be lowered to protect plants against direct sun.*

Growing orchids in a greenhouse

This is the ultimate way to grow orchids and can be the most rewarding, but it is vital to follow a strict daily routine to achieve success. Make sure that the greenhouse stays cool and airy in summer and warm and comfortable in winter; orchids dislike being either cold and wet or hot and dry. You will need to maintain winter temperatures with some form of heating, preferably an electric fan heater rather than fuel-burning heaters, which can cause fumes. Double glaze the windows with clear plastic sheeting to conserve heat. Reduce the temperature in summer, and at other times, by ventilation, shading and damping down, and protect the orchids from direct sun by shading the glass. Use paint-on shading on the outside of the glass and green mesh inside or out. Ventilate the greenhouse whenever possible and leave ventilators open all night during spells of hot weather. Keep up the level of humidity by damping down daily, except in very cold weather, and in summer increase this to twice a day, as well as spraying the orchids overhead. There is no limit to the varieties you can grow in a greenhouse, be they cool, intermediate or warm-growing types. In fact, if it is large enough, you can divide the greenhouse into sections to grow the varieties of your choice.

Right: Shade the greenhouse from early spring to late summer to protect plants and flowers from direct sun. A white paint-on shading will also cool the glass and reduce the inside temperature. Mix this according to the maker's instructions. Use this together with the green mesh shading shown at top.

On aluminum greenhouses, use these special plugs to fix the green mesh shading material a little way from the inside glass.

Keep a check on temperature fluctuations with a thermometer that registers minimum and maximum figures. This will enable you to record how low the temperature drops during the night.

Supply fresh air and control temperatures by opening the top ventilator, but try to avoid causing a cold draft or sudden temperature drop.

Above: *In a small greenhouse a fan to circulate air is a most useful piece of equipment. Position this at staging level to move air through the plants.*

Stand plants at the back of the staging on upturned pots to make it easier to water them.

Fill the staging trays with clay pellets or gravel and top up with water to create humidity. Avoid overcrowding your orchids.

Side ventilation creates a flow of moving air from underneath the plants through to the roof ventilator.

Use a selection of low-light plants, such as ferns, under the staging to improve growing conditions.

Place an electric fan heater at ground level. Warm air will circulate around the greenhouse. Keep the ground wet.

Left: *An ideal set-up for orchids, with plants spaced on staging and hung above. Added greenery underneath the orchids helps to provide the all-important growing environment.*

Points to look out for when buying orchids

If you have never grown orchids before, you may be uncertain of what to buy and where to find stock. Most orchids are sold by specialist orchid nurseries, and it is a good idea to visit one of these to discover the range of orchids available and seek expert advice at the same time. Garden centers and some florists stock a few of the most popular orchids from time to time, but are often limited in the advice they can offer. If you cannot be sure of the conditions required by a plant, you are unlikely to succeed with it. Orchids are available either as young plants, needing several years to bloom, as first-time flowering plants or as large, mature specimens in full bloom. The price will vary according to the age and quality of the plant. Many of the orchid societies formed by enthusiastic amateur growers hold regular plant sales at their meetings and these can be the source of a good bargain. Wherever you obtain your orchids, look for healthy plants that are not in need of immediate repotting. It should not be necessary to check for pests, but aphids occasionally occur even in the best-run establishments. Check that foliage is clean and free from virus. If the plant is in bloom, ensure that the blooms are fresh, so that they will last for many weeks.

Below: *Whether you buy plants in flower or a single cut bloom, make sure that the flowers are fresh enough to last for several weeks.*

A fresh bloom with strong texture to the sepals and petals.

An old bloom showing a reddened lip with loss of texture.

This is a three-year-old plant, with still another year or two of growing to do before it flowers.

A two-year-old seedling, one year out of the flask. It will be two or three years before it flowers.

Right: *For best results, try to buy established plants in pots, growing in a recommended compost. The prices of these miltoniopsis, for example, will vary according to the size of the plants. Always make a point of buying the best plants that you can afford.*

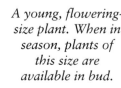

A young, flowering-size plant. When in season, plants of this size are available in bud.

Left: *Commercially grown orchids are sown in sterile flasks. If you see them offered for sale, make sure that the plants are a good dark green and ready to be potted. Plants of this age are difficult for a beginner to handle and may not offer much variety.*

For instant results, look for a mature plant such as this, flowering at its full potential. It will cost more, but provides immediate enjoyment.

Sour-looking compost indicates overwatering.

Small pseudobulbs are an indication that there has been no progression in their growth.

Above: *A poor-looking specimen. This is a sick plant needing specialist care if it is to regain its health. It will be several years before it blooms.*

Below: *When this orchid is removed from its pot, you can see that it has made no roots because the bark has become sour. Do not buy such plants.*

49

Composts & potting

The majority of orchids in cultivation are epiphytes that need open, well-drained compost. The most popular growing medium is non-resinous tree bark. Bark chippings come in different grades for large and small plants, are easy to handle and almost impossible to overwater. Peat is another organic compost, but it holds far more water and can become waterlogged. If it is left dry for long periods while orchids are resting, the acidity of the peat can change when it is watered again, causing roots to die. At one time, osmunda fiber was the basic potting material for all orchids. Today, it is expensive and difficult to obtain, but very useful for growing orchids on cork bark. Some commercially grown orchids are potted in an inert material, such as rockwool, which provides the plant with a moisture base, but you must add all the chemical nutrients and follow a precise feeding formula. If this causes a problem then transfer the plant to an organic compost.

This plant will take a few years to recover if repotted now.

Right: *This Brassia verrucosa has not been repotted for many years and new growths have become increasingly weak. There are stunted roots outside the pot and signs of premature leaf loss on older pseudobulbs. The foliage is paler than normal.*

Orchids root quickly and easily into bark compost. It decomposes slowly, releasing nutrients that provide most of the orchid's requirements. A little extra artificial feed helps to keep plants healthy.

A young plant potted in a fine grade of bark can be 'dropped on' every six months for successive years while the bark remains 'sweet' and in good condition. Chunks of bark provide space for air around the roots. Polystyrene pieces ensure swift drainage.

Peat-based composts can also be used for most terrestrial and semi-terrestrial orchids. These are usually grown in half pots.

Below: *A selection of basic equipment for orchid growing. You can use a variety of containers, with polystyrene for crocking. Plastic pots are available in all sizes. Open, plastic pots for water plants are ideal for suspending the smaller species with roots that grow outside. Plastic hanging baskets accommodate the larger species and are easier to find than the wooden slatted baskets, although these are simple to make yourself. Cork bark is ideal for upward-growing orchids. You will need secateurs and wire to secure a plant onto cork, and bamboo canes, string, labels, pen, leaf wipes and a pruning knife. Keep methylated spirits, a toothbrush and scissors to hand for pest control. Colored labels help you to code your orchids, e.g. red to rest, blue to water, etc. This system is particularly useful in the winter.*

Rockwool and polystyrene granules provide an inorganic compost for this plant. As they have no food value, you must supply all the nutrients. The soft, open mix encourages quick root growth. Do not pack the rockwool too firmly and, ideally, wear a face mask to filter out any dry fibers in the air.

A compost made up of Finnish peat. Foam rubber pieces and polystyrene are added as aggregates to give more space and to aid swift drainage when watering.

51

Watering, spraying & feeding

Orchids need watering and spraying throughout their growing period. Some grow all year round, while others rest in winter. Plants often bloom while resting. Resting orchids require just enough water to keep the pseudobulbs from shriveling. A plant is resting between the formation of its last pseudobulb and the appearance of the next new growth, which may take a few weeks or several months. Orchids with short resting periods should be watered all year; do not let them dry out.

Spraying is another way of providing moisture, but does not take the place of watering. Daily spraying during spring and summer helps to cool the foliage during hot weather, deters pests and maintains humidity around the plants. Water and spray in the early part of the day when the temperature is rising. The leaves should be dry by the time the temperature starts to drop towards nightfall. Avoid spraying buds and flowers. Orchids will benefit from a light feed during their growing season. Those that grow all year round need less feed in winter and more in summer. You can apply the feed directly to the roots or spray it over the foliage. Use a specially formulated orchid feed according to the maker's instructions. As a general rule, feed the orchids at every second or third watering. The clear water will wash out any residue and prevents potentially harmful overfeeding.

Orchid feed is available in powder, granular or liquid form. If you use a general plant feed, mix it to the weakest recommended concentration.

Above: *For orchids in bark, light feeding will supplement natural nutrients. In rockwool, an inert growing medium, regular feeding is important.*

Right: *Use a spouted watering can to flood the surface, giving the plant plenty of water at one application. Most of it will run directly through the compost.*

Below: *If a plant has become too dry, place it in a bowl of water and leave it to soak for up to one hour. You may need to hold it down for a while.*

Right: *In tropical rainforests, many orchids grow on trees and are drenched with rain each day. In a greenhouse, you can use a spray lance to imitate this effect.*

When spraying the foliage, avoid getting water onto the flowers, which can cause damp spots to appear.

Keep the water slightly below the base of the plant so that it does not get into the new growths and to prevent loose compost from floating away.

Below: *Indoors, you must spray with more care. Use a hand-held spray bottle to mist the plant with water or a feed.*

Common growing problems

Common growing problems are the result of incorrect culture, which cause the orchid to show one or more signs of stress. Most problems are caused by extremes of heat and dryness that can build up in a greenhouse in summer or cold and wet in winter. Orchids with an overall yellowing of their foliage are suffering either from too much light or insufficient feeding. Increase the shading over them and use a nitrogen-based feed. The loss of the occasional leaf from the oldest pseudobulbs is natural, but a premature loss of leaves can be caused either by poisoning from fuel-burning heater fumes, root loss or extremes of heat or cold. Repot the plants as soon as possible, cutting out dead roots and old pseudobulbs. Shriveled pseudobulbs or limp foliage may be the result of under- or overwatering. Pseudobulbs become shriveled from lack of moisture and if roots are lost through overwatering, the result is the same. Given increased moisture, the underwatered plant will plump up again within weeks, but overwatered plants should be repotted and may take one or two years to recover. Dehydration of the foliage is also the result of incorrect watering; spraying the leaves helps prevent further moisture loss. Black tips or spotting on leaves are more often associated with low temperatures. It is false economy to grow orchids below the recommended minimum temperature, as this encourages fungal infections and problems with rotting.

Spray dehydrated leaves more often to help them regain their natural texture.

Shriveled pseudobulbs will plump up again when new roots appear from the young growth.

1 *An example of die back on a cattleya leaf caused by cold conditions. Cut off the affected part using a sharp, sterilized knife.*

2 *Using a cotton bud or paintbrush, carefully dust the cut with yellow sulfur to dry up the wound. Keep the affected area dry for a few days.*

Use yellow sulfur for all types of plant wounds.

Below: *Pseudobulbs should be plump at all times. Shriveling will result from under- or overwatering, or after repotting before new roots appear. Pseudobulbs may also become shriveled for a short time after a period of heavy flowering.*

Glossy, firm-textured leaves shine with good health.

Plump pseudobulbs will ensure an increase in the size of the next season's growth.

This plant has been overwatered and shows signs of premature leaf loss and leaf die-back. It will have no live roots.

A healthy plant should look like this. There is glossy, green foliage on all the pseudobulbs and their size increases each year. There are live roots in the pot.

Above: *Two cymbidiums - a healthy plant on the right and a weakened plant with growing problems on the left. The dying plant is unlikely to recover at this stage. Sadly, there is little alternative but to discard it.*

Right: *Exposure to direct sun will very quickly burn orchid leaves. This can easily happen in early spring before the greenhouse shading has been put in place. Placing sheets of newspaper over the plants will protect them until the shading is in position. (See page 46 for advice on shading a greenhouse.)*

1 *Cut any black tips off leaves to prevent the die back from continuing to run back down the leaf. Use sterilized gardening tools.*

2 *Rather than cutting them square, trim leaf ends at an angle. This makes them look more natural and improves the appearance of the orchid.*

If this Coelogyne has further spare 'eyes' at the base of the pseudobulbs, it means that more new growth will appear.

If water collects in the top or hollow part of young growths, it will cause them to rot and eventually die.

Left: Premature ageing or spotting of flowers can be the result of too much light or, as shown here, of water being sprayed directly onto the flowers. Low temperatures will have a similar effect.

Plump pseudobulbs, glossy foliage, strong new growth and a flower spike are all signs of a healthy plant.

Left: To save a plant in this condition, separate each pseudobulb and treat them as propagations. Where there are dormant 'eyes', they will grow.

Below: *Two potted vuylstekearas. The one on the left is a healthy, growing, flowering plant, while the one on the right is ailing. Note the difference in condition of pseudobulbs and foliage.*

Signs of neglect are corrugations on leaves, dryness in the early stage of growth, shriveled pseudobulbs and new growth dying back. ·

Below: *Bud drop is a common condition caused by a sudden change in growing conditions. The buds turn yellow and drop off.*

These buds have been affected by fluctuations in temperature or lighting.

Normal buds should develop like this.

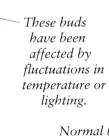

1 Basal rot has spread from a black, warty depression on the pseudobulb. Remove the pseudobulb by severing the rhizome to prevent rot from spreading.

2 The severed pseudobulb has a healthy, white rhizome at the base. A brown or black rhizome would indicate that the rot had spread further.

A large depression has shrunk one side of this pseudobulb, causing it to become deformed.

Another dried-up blister is visible here. Cut the blister to release the liquid. Dry and pack the wound with sulfur.

3 Keep a careful watch on a plant such as this in case basal rot reappears in another pseudobulb. They are all affected by black depressions - originally water-filled blisters - caused by cold and damp conditions.

Basal rot affects some of the Oncidium species. This plant is O. leucochilum.

Pests & diseases

Few pests or diseases are specific to orchids. Most pests are commonly found on other plants as well, and treatments for controlling them are available at garden centers. As many orchid collections are small and often kept in the home, it is safer to avoid chemical remedies. The non-chemical treatments suggested here will clean the plants of existing pests as they appear. For longer term prevention, apply a systemic insecticide that renders the plant poisonous to the pest. Be sure to use such products in accordance with the manufacturer's instructions. Remember that in the home or greenhouse, pests can arrive from outside, surviving through the winter in the warm conditions. Check plants frequently for pests to prevent the build-up of large colonies which, once established, can be extremely difficult to eradicate. Most of the pests that plague orchids are the sap-sucking mites and insects. They damage the leaf tissues and spread virus disease by moving from plant to plant. The most common disease found on orchids is cymbidium mosaic virus, which appears on orchids under stress. Plants weakened through neglect or insect infestation are most at risk. There is no cure for virus disease, so ideally you should destroy affected plants or at least isolate them from other orchids.

These black aphids, or blackfly, occur on buds and flowers, usually on the undersides of sepals and petals, and cause ageing of blooms. Swill flowers in a bowl of water with a little detergent or dislodge the aphids with a fine water jet.

Do not use an aphid repellent aerosol on buds or flowers; it can cause yellowing and bud drop.

These white clusters are where the eggs are laid and will hatch.

Yellow patches show damage by scale insects.

The eggs hatch into mobile insects that move off to become settled adults under their shells.

There are various types of scale insects.

Scale insects occur mainly on the undersides of leaves and beneath bracts, where they cover pseudobulbs.

Right: *Scale insects on a cattleya leaf. There are different types of scale insect, all extremely small and covered with a scaly membrane that may be white or brownish. Scale can be hard or soft.*

Above: *Black aphids, or blackfly, are particularly persistent and develop into a swarm within a matter of days. As they are smaller than green aphids, or greenfly, they can be difficult to spot in isolated numbers at the outset.*

Right: If left unchecked, large numbers of aphids will attack buds, flowers and young growths. Young growths can turn yellow and, in severe cases, areas of leaf die off and become deformed. Buds will also be deformed, turn yellow and drop off.

Below: Treat scale and other sucking insects with methylated spirits, either neat or diluted in water on soft leaves. The pests are killed on contact and you can dislodge them with a toothbrush. Rinse the plant in water to prevent marking.

Wash aphids off with water and detergent or use a cotton bud dipped in methylated spirits on isolated pests. Alternatively, use an aerosol spray on foliage.

Do not confuse the natural brown flecking on this plant - Acineta densa - with damage.

Below: *Red spider mite is one of the commonest pests and also one of the most difficult to see. Use leaf wipes to clean both sides of the leaves and look at the leaf wipe through a magnifying glass to detect evidence of the pests.*

Look for discoloration on the undersides of leaves. In the early stage, red spider mite damage shows up as whitish areas, which later turn black. Treat as for scale insects.

The damaged area on a young bud will grow as the bud develops, spoiling the eventual bloom.

Left: *Slugs and snails can cause considerable harm to all parts of the plant. Although they prefer the softer buds and root tips, they will also chew pseudobulbs. Treat such wounds with yellow sulfur, as shown on page 54.*

Protect buds with a slug repellent before they reach this stage.

The streaking caused by cymbidium mosaic virus is quite different from other markings. There is no cure for the virus, but improved culture can sometimes arrest it.

Above: *Mealybugs, a group of scale insects with white filamentlike hairs, are sometimes confused with woolly scale. They can occur on all parts of the plant, but usually where flower stems join the main stem. They cause yellowing and deformity of developing buds and spikes.*

Right: *Cymbidium mosaic virus will show up as distinct diamond-patterned streaks along the leaf surface. In the early stage, the streaks appear as pale flecking, but later on these markings will turn black.*

Keeping plants looking good

Taking a pride in the general appearance of your orchids is important if plants are to look good all year round. It also ensures that you quickly spot any pests that appear and can deal with them promptly. Greenhouse plants need an annual overhaul, say at repotting time. Remove dead back bulbs and any dead leaves that occur naturally from time to time. Do not allow leaves to decay on the bench, which encourages pests. In the home or conservatory, discreet ties can support broken or bending leaves, and split canes usually improve the angle of developing flower spikes. You can also use canes to control unmanageable pseudobulbs on cattleyas and dendrobiums, which may otherwise become top heavy, causing damage if they fall. Many orchids produce a protective sheathing that covers the young pseudobulbs and flower spikes as they progress. Once fully developed, the plant sheds this sheath, which turns brown. At this stage you can remove the sheaths from pseudobulbs to encourage end-of-season ripening, and from flower stems to prevent pests from harboring there.

Above: Remove yellow leaves when they are 'ripe' enough to be picked easily from the plant. This is safer than cutting, which can spread virus disease when tools are used on another plant.

Above: Use leaf wipes or clean water to sponge foliage that has become dulled with hard water or residue from insecticides. It should not be necessary to use leaf shine on orchids.

There is a clear line on the green leaf showing where it will eventually come away from the bract above the pseudobulb.

Remove dried bracts by splitting one at a time down each side of the pseudobulb and pulling away.

1 Cymbidium pseudobulbs that have shed their leaves are left with sharp, spiny bracts at the base. These look unsightly and can harbor pests, so remove them as shown here.

2 If you remove the bracts at the right stage, it will be quite easy for you to pull them away without causing any injury to the pseudobulbs.

Some of these back bulbs are surplus to the plant's requirements. The three in the foreground can be removed for propagation.

3 Once the back bulbs have been stripped of their bracts, they not only look better but will also receive more light to speed up ripening.

1 *Cymbidium leaves are long-lived and can become damaged, spoiling the general look of the plant. Instead of cutting the leaves off, you can easily repair them using green string. In time, the string can be removed and the leaves will support themselves.*

2 *Use the undamaged center leaves to hold the outside leaves in place. Place the string around the center leaves and tie a knot.*

The center leaves are strong enough to provide a support for the damaged leaves.

3 *Bring each leaf in turn towards the string tie and wrap the string around the leaf to hold it in position. Alternatively, use pieces of raffia.*

4 *Twist the string in between each leaf. There is no need to tie a knot behind every leaf; it will only make the string difficult to remove later on.*

5 *Finally, tie a knot behind the last leaf and cut off any surplus string. The finished repair can stay in place as long as the leaves remain on the plant.*

6 *Within a few months, you can carefully remove the string or raffia and the repaired leaves will once again be able to support themselves.*

Basic potting methods - dropping on

Dropping on is the easiest method of repotting an orchid. It simply involves taking a plant from its outgrown pot and placing it in a larger one without disturbing the root ball. It causes the minimum of disruption to the plant and can therefore be done at almost any time of the year. It is a good way for beginners to practice the potting technique and gain confidence before tackling the other methods featured on pages 68-75. Dropping on is ideal for young plants, and also for larger ones that are not ready for division. Orchids can be dropped on repeatedly for a number of years until the compost becomes completely decomposed and useless. It is important to use a compost that matches the one in which the plant is already growing. Mixing two composts in one pot can lead to watering problems later on, as one type may be more porous and therefore need less water than the other.

A plant can be dropped on provided that it is healthy and growing well, with the majority of its pseudobulbs in leaf. It may need repotting because it has outgrown its pot or used up most of the food supply. When you remove the plant you should have a strong root system with live roots distributed evenly throughout the compost, binding it into a solid ball. The compost should be in good condition, not totally decomposed, and if containing bark, it should have a pleasant damp, woody aroma. Before dropping on, allow your plant to partially dry out. You can water it within a day or two of potting.

1 *Ease the plant from the pot by squeezing it until the plant becomes loose and lifts out. Otherwise, cut the pot away. Notice the healthy roots here.*

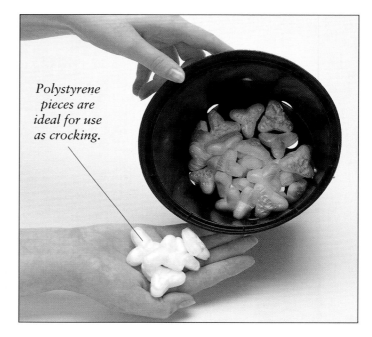

Polystyrene pieces are ideal for use as crocking.

2 *Select a clean pot 2in(5cm) larger in diameter than the original one. Place just sufficient crocking material in the pot to cover the base. This will help to ensure good drainage.*

Hold the plant steady with one hand and pour handfuls of compost into the pot with the other. This bark has been dampened before use.

Make sure that the base of the plant is slightly below, and not above, the rim of the pot.

Add more compost until the pot is full, not forgetting the sides.

3 Position your plant carefully in the new pot, leaving room at the front for it to grow forward. To do this, place the oldest pseudobulbs against one side of the pot.

Plastic pots are more popular than clay ones, because they are lighter, easier to use and non-porous.

4 Firm the compost by pressing it with your fingers around the rim of the pot, pushing it well down all round.

5 If the potting has been firm, you should be able to lift the plant as shown here without the pot falling off. If this test fails, firm the compost again using more pressure.

6 Firm potting is essential if the plant is to continue growing well for the next two years. Finally, do remember to replace the label; at this stage, many plants look alike!

Basic potting methods - repotting

The method of repotting a cymbidium featured here shows the standard procedure that can be followed for most orchids. Ideally, carry this out during the spring when the new growths are up to about 10cm(4in) long and before they have started to make their new roots. Repotting at the right stage of growth and at the ideal time of the year enables the plant to make a swift recovery with the minimum interruption to its growing cycle.

Repotting is an opportunity to clean out all the old, decomposed and exhausted compost from under the plant. It also allows you to remove any old roots that have died naturally and any surplus back bulbs. You can often save the back bulbs and use them to propagate a further plant (see page 85). Plants that have become too large can be divided where appropriate. You can split plants where sections with at least four pseudobulbs and a new growth can be kept as intact pieces. All or most of these pseudobulbs should be active and in leaf. If they are dormant, out of leaf back bulbs you will need to divide them singly to encourage them to grow.

Repot plants while they are on the dry side. After repotting, do not water them for a few days to allow trimmed or broken roots time to heal and prevent any risk of rotting. But you can spray the foliage and compost to prevent moisture loss during this period.

This is the back of the plant where the oldest (and smallest) pseudobulbs are. The plant will not produce new growth from here.

This is the new growth at the front of the plant. After repotting, this is where the new roots will come from.

The compost has largely broken down and has been replaced by the extensive roots. Note how thick and fleshy they are.

1 The vigorous root system of this plant contains both living and dead roots. There are several pseudobulbs but the plant is not large enough to divide and there are no surplus back bulbs to remove.

2 *Starting underneath, remove the crocks and all the old compost. Tease out the roots and shake the plant to release the compost. You may need to cut some roots to separate them.*

3 *Dead roots are dry and hollow. These are at the back and need to be cut away. Trim the live roots to a length of about 6in(15cm). If left long, these roots will snap and cause rotting.*

Place a handful or two of compost on top of the crocking to bring the plant to the correct level in the pot. Fill in with compost while holding the plant steady.

4 *Using a new pot 2in(5cm) larger than the old one, position the plant with room in the front for new growth. Fold the roots underneath until the plant rests just below the pot rim.*

Basic potting methods - dividing

It is not always essential to divide orchids once they reach a certain size. If you prefer, you can grow them into specimen plants, with the majority of pseudobulbs in leaf. This is a good strategy with the smaller species, if they are to reach their full potential. However, the larger orchids, such as cymbidiums and cattleyas, can become unmanageable if allowed to reach their maximum size and may outgrow the space allocated to them. A good time to divide a plant is when it has grown in two or more directions at the same time and its irregular shape will not allow it to fit easily into a larger pot. A new pot would have to be so large that the result would be overpotting, and overwatering would become unavoidable. Sometimes, the middle of a plant contains a surplus of leafless back bulbs. Remove these to prevent them from becoming a strain on the plant. Cutting away such unwanted back bulbs is an easy way of dividing the plant into pieces. Do make sure that each piece has at least four pseudobulbs on it; very small divisions will reduce the plant's flowering ability until it has regained its vigor, which could take two or three years. Dividing has several advantages. Not only do you reduce the size of the plant, but you also increase your stock and create 'spare' plants to exchange with fellow enthusiasts. Alternatively, you may prefer to keep the extra plants and try growing them in different positions. This is a useful tactic when a plant has been reluctant to bloom.

All these pseudobulbs are in leaf, with no surplus back bulbs to remove.

1 *This* Laelia autumnalis *has grown in two directions. Repotting would mean overpotting it, unless you place it in an oblong basket. It is an ideal candidate for dividing.*

If the plant had been repotted before these new roots had grown, there would be no risk of damaging them as you divide the plant.

On this pseudobulb, this year's roots have not yet started to grow, which is an advantage.

2 *Out of its pot, you can see how orchids make roots in and out of the compost. Aerial roots will not grow in compost; new underground ones will grow.*

Use a sharp knife to make a clean cut through the rhizome.

Take care to avoid slicing into the base of the fleshy pseudobulbs.

It is impossible to avoid damaging these young growing roots. New ones will appear soon after repotting.

It should be easy to pull apart the two halves. If necessary, cut through the roots.

3 As you divide the plant, leave a minimum of four pseudobulbs on each division to avoid reducing the flowering ability of the plant. Smaller divisions than this will take several years to reach flowering size. Separate the plant by cutting vertically through the rhizome joining the pseudobulbs, using a sharp knife sterilized by dipping it in methylated spirits.

Stand plants with their new growths facing forwards, so that you can observe their progress. Replace labels at the back.

4 Now you can pot up the two halves in suitably sized pots, as described on pages 68-69. Some shriveling may occur before new growths and roots appear. In the meantime, keep moist and spray well.

Basic potting methods - using a hanging basket

Many of the epiphytic species can be grown in hanging baskets. This is particularly useful for orchids that like plenty of light because you can hang them in the roof of the greenhouse or conservatory. It also allows roots with a tendency to grow outside the pot to trail at will, causing less of a problem than when they attach themselves to the staging. Orchids with a rambling or untidy habit can often be more easily accommodated in a basket. Bulbophyllums, for example, will often grow in 'heaps', new pseudobulbs being made on top of others. After a few years, the plant will completely encompass the basket, growing all round to form a tight ball. When this occurs, repotting without breaking up the plant becomes impossible. One method of renewing compost is simply to tuck fresh bark, or similar, in among the heaped pseudobulbs. Because of their sometimes long, pendent flower spikes, gongoras and stanhopeas also lend themselves to growing in baskets. Stanhopeas produce their flower spikes from the side or base of the basket. Baskets may be the round plastic type or wooden slatted ones, either square, oblong or diamond-shaped. Or, of course, you can make your own.

1 *This* Brassia *is long overdue for repotting. It has many leafless pseudobulbs and is large enough to be divided and planted in a basket.*

This is the strongest and most vigorous of the two pieces.

2 *Cut through the rhizome joining the oldest back bulbs. The resulting two independent plants can be treated separately.*

These back bulbs are badly shriveled, but still alive. The newer pseudobulbs have almost exhausted them. Some may still grow if you pot them up separately.

Most of these older roots are dead, with only the thin, inner core remaining. Cut them away, leaving enough for anchorage.

Trim these live aerial roots back to about 6in(15cm).

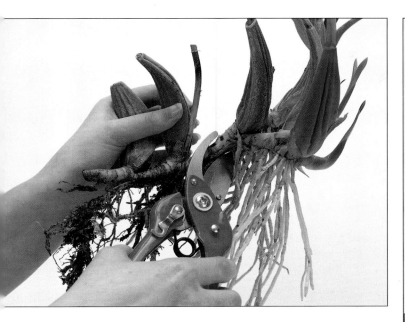

3 Restore the balance of this plant by removing two back bulbs to leave three pseudobulbs (one out of leaf) and two new growths. Cut the woody rhizome between the pseudobulbs.

4 Having selected a basket, line it with netting to retain the planting compost. Position the plant diagonally across the basket to give it maximum room, tucking the roots underneath.

5 Compared with the plant shown at the beginning of the sequence, this orchid is clearly much more comfortable. Attach plastic string or wire to the basket so that you can hang it up. If using string, add a small metal hook at the top.

One or two older leaves will turn yellow and drop off. The new growths will make up the loss.

Buried aerial roots may not survive. New roots from young growths will soon appear.

Basic potting methods - *using a piece of cork*

There are many advantages to growing orchids on slabs of bark. The epiphytic species often grow better this way and it is easier to contain orchids with a climbing habit. Aerial roots can be encouraged and, because you are able to see the roots growing, you are more aware of the plant's needs. There will be less need to disturb the plants and you can save valuable bench room by hanging them at either end of your greenhouse or conservatory. Do not grow orchids on bark indoors, however, because the atmosphere is too dry for aerial roots to progress satisfactorily. You can expand on this basic idea by attaching orchids to tree branches to form an attractive permanent display. Use cork bark that is slow to rot and has a rough surface, or choose some other hard wood, such as oak or apple. Avoid resinous pines. When a plant outgrows its piece of bark, either transfer it to a longer piece of bark or reduce its size by removing back bulbs so that you can reuse the same piece of bark. Orchids growing in this way will dry out faster than in a pot, so drench them daily by thorough spraying. Otherwise, dip them in water to keep them moist. Spray the foliage and roots regularly, taking care not to get water in the new growth.

This cork slab is large enough to accommodate the plant for three or four years.

1 *Insert wire through the bark and make into a hook. Place dampened osmunda fiber in position on the cork. If unavailable, use live sphagnum moss or a similar absorbent material.*

Cork bark slab

Osmunda fiber

Prepared Brassia *plant*

Wire for making hook

Plant label

Plastic-coated wire

Small pliers

To attach the plant, pass the wire between the pseudobulbs, drawing it across the hard rhizome.

2 Position the plant so that the back bulbs are placed at the bottom end, leaving as much room as possible at the top for future pseudobulbs to grow. It is a good idea to extend the fiber to the top of the bark so that the plant can grow into it.

3 You will need two or three lengths of wire to hold the plant with its osmunda pad firmly in place. Use the pliers to tighten the wire, but do not let it press into the pseudobulbs.

4 As soon as you have finished attaching the plant to the cork, spray the plant and its osmunda base. Keep both moist to encourage the new roots, which will appear very soon.

Label the plant clearly. Adding the date can be helpful for future reference.

BRASSIA MACULATA

5 The final result is a plant firmly attached to the bark, with room to develop. Trim any untidy strands of osmunda to give a professional finish.

75

Staking methods
- a cattleya

Large brassocattleyas can produce three or four blooms on one stem, each bloom measuring 5in(13cm) across. The blooms may become top heavy and unable to support themselves, flopping forward and possibly snapping under their own weight. Staking, therefore, gives the blooms support and allows each one to be seen to best advantage. Staking can improve the position of a single bloom or any number on one stem. The best time to stake cattleyas is at the advanced bud stage or when the blooms have first opened and are fresh. Bear in mind that most species have sufficient natural support to hold their blooms erect, and the many miniature types in this group will require little or no staking. The staking method described here is also suitable for single-stem blooming orchids, including lycastes, anguloas and their hybrids, and the large-flowered maxillarias. Thin, green bamboo splits are less obtrusive than ordinary bamboo canes for staking and you can cut them with a pair of secateurs. Sharpen one end of the cane into a point, before inserting it into the compost in an upright position, close to the plant and away from the rim of the pot where most of the roots are. This will cause minimum damage to the orchid's root system.

If you are using one central cane, place another tie around the top of the pseudobulb.

Measure length of cane from below the pot rim to the top of the bloom and cut it off. You can raise or turn individual blooms to enhance their appearance.

2 Using the secateurs, carefully, make a split about 2in(5cm) in the top of the cane. This will be sufficient to hold the flower stem in place.

1 Some cattleyas will require one central cane to hold the main stem. Where this is all that is needed, you can cut the cane to the required length so that it does not show above the blooms when the main stem is tied to it.

Shape this end of the cane into a point so that it causes less damage to roots when pushed into the compost.

3 Position the cane upright in the compost, close to the plant and just behind the bloom. If you intend to raise the bloom, make sure that the cane is long enough to support it or lift the cane slightly out of the pot.

4 Hold the split end of the cane open, lift the bloom carefully and lower it so that the stem rests in the top of the cane. The bloom should now be secure in the top of the cane.

5 Once the bloom is held firmly by the cane, you can lift or lower it as required. By twisting the cane, you can turn the bloom to the left or to the right. If you turn this bloom, all three flowers will face in the same direction.

If necessary, insert an individual cane to hold this bloom in position.

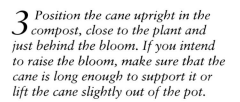

Right: To achieve the ideal presentation of cattleya blooms, each one should face outwards to form a semicircle. The blooms may touch one another, but they should not overlap.

Staking methods - an odontoglossum

The method of staking a flower spike described here also applies to a range of other orchids that produce long, multiflowered spikes. Cymbidiums, zygopetalums and phalaenopsis will all benefit from being trained in this way. Staking keeps flower spikes upright or semi-arching, and prevents heavily budded cymbidium spikes from snapping under their own weight. Start training cymbidium spikes when the spike is about 6in (15cm) long and growing rapidly. By tying it to a cane at this stage and increasing the ties as it grows, you will encourage it to become upright and straight. Keep the string ties below the budded portion to enable the end of the spike to arch naturally if this is its habit. Odontoglossum spikes usually grow straight up and need not be trained until quite advanced. Phalaenopsis spikes can be more wayward, but are easily controlled at an early stage.

3 Insert the pointed cane into the compost as close to the flower spike as possible. Avoid the rim of the pot, where most of the roots will be.

If you prefer an upright effect, use a longer cane and extra ties.

One tie here is all that is required to support this flower spike.

2 In most cases, it will only be necessary to support the flower spike to the base of the buds. Cut the cane accordingly, allowing a little extra to be pushed into the compost.

1 The advantages of staking flower spikes are clearly illustrated here. Unsupported spikes grow at an angle and are easily broken or damaged.

If tied up too late - when these advanced buds have become set - the flowers will open sideways on the stem.

4 Loop string around the cane while holding up the flower spike to bring it close to the string. Hold the spike this way to test its flexibility. Most spikes are quite supple.

5 Twist the string between the cane and spike. Leave the string loose enough so that the developing spike can continue to grow and you can move the string higher as necessary.

6 When you have finished, the spike should be clear of the cane to prevent any bruising, which may occur with delicate spikes, such as phalaenopsis.

Flowers tied upright can become bunched and the overall effect is less attractive and unnatural. However, if the spike is on one side of the pot, tying it upright will prevent the plant toppling over.

An arching spray of flowers looks more attractive and the blooms will be better spaced on the stem.

Young plants with only a few blooms flowering for the first time will not require staking.

7 Successful staking starts when the flower spike is young. Some orchids need the minimum of support, while others require training throughout their development.

Avoid placing canes close to new growths; they could impede plant development.

Staking methods - a paphiopedilum

Paphiopedilums have very powerful flowers that could be described as mesmeric. Their unique characteristics and petal formation set them apart from other orchids, and staking their flowers correctly can only enhance these qualities. Generally, unstaked paphiopedilums will open their flowers shyly, drooping forward so that only the top of the flower is visible. In the wild, this prevents water from filling the pouch, which is shielded by the dorsal sepal. In cultivation, however, the aim is to view the whole flower. The blooms on some paphiopedilums, particularly the green-leaved varieties, can be remarkably heavy. Without some support, their weight can dislodge the plant, pulling it sideways out of the pot by the roots. The weight of the blooms causes flower stems to grow out almost at right angles, lying across the plant. The method of staking described here can be used for both green-leaved and mottled varieties, and also other single-flowered orchids. Those with multi-flowered spikes, such as *Paphiopedilum rothschildianum*, and the taller-stemmed phragmipediums, require similar staking, but without the additional tie attached behind the flower.

Unstaked flowers will lean over and droop forward. Long slender stems can become bent.

This plant is being pulled out of its pot by the weight of the flower.

When the flower stem is brought back to the cane it will be in an upright position.

1 *Begin staking the plant when the stem is several inches high. Tie the stem loosely to a thin split cane. As the stem lengthens, you can move the tie along the stem to maintain support.*

2 *Here, the flower has opened. Now take a split cane that is just shorter than the bloom and place it as close as possible to the flower stem in an upright position. It will serve to hold both the plant and flower steady.*

3 Take a length of green string and loop it behind the flower at the very top of the stem. Twist the string and pull it gently towards the cane until it is tight enough.

Drawing the bloom back towards the cane has raised it sufficiently to be seen full face.

4 Tie the string, making sure that the stem has sufficient space to develop. Cut the ends of the string off with scissors to make a neat finish.

If necessary, use extra support ties along the length of the stem. The number will vary according to the stem size.

5 When the bloom has been open for a few days and has become set, you can put the last tie in position behind the flower. If you tie it back too soon, the bloom will resume its natural habit and droop forward. You will then find it difficult to bring the bloom back into position.

Propagating orchids - *natural methods*

A few orchids will propagate themselves without any inducement from you and when this happens, it is an ideal opportunity to grow on another plant. Although it will be two to three years before most propagations reach flowering size, the wait is well worthwhile. Raising orchids from seed is not easy for the home grower, so bringing on young propagations is both rewarding and satisfying. Natural propagation occurs when a plant produces a 'kiki', or young plant, either from the top of a dormant pseudobulb, as in some encyclias and zygopetalums, for example, or from the base of a dormant pseudobulb, as in cymbidiums and occasionally odontoglossums, etc. Phalaenopsis are unique in producing the occasional 'kiki' on a flowering stem. Such propagations can occur not only on healthy plants, but also on sick ones, where new growths have died and there are no more dormant eyes at the base. Pleiones are especially prolific at propagating themselves; one species, *Pleione humilus*, will produce dozens of tiny bulblets from the top of the previous year's pseudobulb. These can be left in place until potting time in the spring. The bulblets are very small and need careful handling, but all can be encouraged to grow by placing them together in a community pot. By far the most easily propagated group are the dendrobiums. Their propagation is affected by culture, particularly those of the *nobile* type, which bloom along the length of their canes after resting. If watered too early, the embryo buds will turn into growths instead.

Above: Dendrobium *Sailor Boy, one of the fine hybrids raised from* Dendrobium nobile. *These orchids propagate themselves easily.*

Remove the individual plants when they have made their first pseudobulb and have their own roots. The next new growth may already be showing at the base. Cut the old cane about 1in(2.5cm) from the last plantlet, using a sharp knife between the nodes.

1 Dendrobium nobile, *showing the 'kikis' that have grown along the length of a mature cane, or pseudobulb. These little plants appeared in the spring at the expense of flowers. Leave them on the stem until the following spring.*

Dust the severed ends with sulfur to dry up the area and prevent any rotting.

The piece of old cane left attached will help to anchor the plantlet when it is potted.

Be sure to label the young plants correctly at this stage. If they need support, stake them with short canes.

2 Separate each little plant by slicing through the old cane behind the propagation, leaving a slither of cane still attached to the plantlet. This will prevent damage to the base of the new plant. Alternatively, cut the cane into sections, each with a plantlet attached. Dust all cuts with powdered sulfur.

3 Pot the propagations in small pots using a fine bark compost or similar alternative. Be careful not to pot too deeply. The base of the plant should be on top of the compost and not below it. The new growths, which will come from the base, must start above ground, otherwise they will rot.

Propagating orchids - induced methods

1 *To propagate Dendrobium nobile and similar orchids, select a large, leafless, but unflowered, mature cane. Leave at least four canes on the plant.*

This is an unflowered cane that will produce growths from the nodes.

Using secateurs, cut the cane off at the base and dust the severed end with yellow sulfur.

Propagation can be induced at repotting time, when surplus pseudobulbs have been removed from the plant, by encouraging these old, dormant pseudobulbs to grow. First check that the pseudobulbs are hard and green under the bracts and then look for live dormant eyes around the base, which appear as small, brown triangular swellings. Cymbidiums are among the most easily propagated from old pseudobulbs, but propagating odontoglossum types is more risky and involves cutting off the leading pseudobulb. It is more difficult to induce propagation in vandas and phalaenopsis, as they usually produce new growth from the base only when the main plant has rotted or become damaged at the center. Stem propagation in phalaenopsis sometimes occurs naturally, but it also be induced by coating the nodes on the flowered stem with a hormone paste, which encourages new growth instead of a secondary stem of flowers. Propagate cattleyas by severing the back rhizome while it is still in the pot, a year before repotting. When the plant is eventually repotted, the back bulbs will have begun to grow.

2 *Divide the cane into several pieces of equal length, leaving two nodes on each piece. With orchids such as Dendrobium phalaenopsis, use only the top of the cane, where the eyes are.*

The nodes are small swellings opposite the base of the old leaf bract and covered by it.

3 Prepare a community pot with living sphagnum moss or other moisture-retaining material. Dip each end of the cut pieces of cane into yellow sulfur and place the cuttings around the edge of the flower pot.

4 Make sure the nodes are level with the moss, so that new growths will develop above the surface. Pack extra moss into the pot until the cane pieces are firmly in place.

Keep the moss moist and place the pot in a propagating frame until new growths are established.

HOW THE NEW PLANTS DEVELOP

Inset: A newly potted back bulb from *Brassia maculata*. Keep compost moist to encourage growth, which should show within six weeks. The parent back bulb can remain attached to the new plant until it dies or until the new plant has three pseudobulbs and is independent.

Main photo: A propagation of *Coelogyne*, showing two new pseudobulbs that have grown from a back bulb. The new pseudobulbs are smaller. Within another year, this propagation could reach flowering size.

Pollinating orchids

It is not easy for the hobby grower to raise orchids from seed; at best you will succeed in raising just a very few plants. Commercial orchid growers raise their plants from seed sown in sterile flasks, in a solution containing nutrients that encourage successful germination and growth. This compares with the natural world, where the orchid seed requires the support of a specific mycorrhiza, or microscopic fungus, to initiate development in a symbiotic relationship. However, effecting pollination and obtaining seed is not difficult, and the experience of watching a large seed capsule develop is well worthwhile. This is not unusual in a greenhouse where bees have had access. Some commercial nurseries will be happy to sow your seed for you, usually on the basis of sharing the resulting seedlings and returning just as many as you require. Make enquiries before pollinating and take expert advice on which blooms to use. If you decide to raise your own orchids, select two parent plants of the same genus or, with odontoglossums and cattleyas, a related genus. Look for quality of bloom and color. Then select the stronger of the two plants to be the 'female' and carry the seed capsule. Use the first flower on the stem of the other plant to contribute the pollen, making sure the flower is fresh and that the pollen is intact. Orchid pollen is solid and generally forms two, golden yellow masses attached to the column.

3 Hold the flower steady with one hand. With the other, carefully place the point of the cane under the pollen and lift up. The pollen will come away, attached to the cane by a sticky patch. This basic method is the same in all orchids, except the paphiopedilums and related genera. Their pollen is found on either side of the central column.

1 You can see the pollen cap, or anther, at the end of the central column. Use a thin pointed cane to lift up the pollen cap and it will fall away to reveal the two pollen masses.

2 Check that the pollen is golden yellow. If it is brown or black it has rotted. Possibly the bloom is too old and you will need to select another, younger flower.

Place the cane with pollens attached carefully on one side. Use another cane to remove the anther and pollen from the second flower.

4 *Your second flower will be the capsule, or pod, bearer. Repeat the process of removing anther and pollen and place the cane on one side. Pick up the first cane to transfer the pollen.*

Press the pollen onto the stigma located on the underside of the column. Hold the lip down for easy access.

Pull the cane up and it will come away, leaving the pollen stuck to the stigma. Pollination is then complete.

Raising orchid seed

If everything has gone well at the pollination stage, the flower should show red flushing on the lip before shriveling up, and the stem immediately behind the flower will start to swell. When the remaining flowers on the stem have faded, cut the spike well above the developing seed capsule. Over the next five to nine months, depending upon the type, the capsule will continue to swell and finally ripen. If a nurseryman is to sow your seed by the artificial method, he will require the unopened capsule while the seed is still sterile. Otherwise, select a 'mother' plant, prepare the soil surface as a fine seedbed and water it well. Now watch out for the yellowing and splitting of the capsule and, as soon as this occurs, slit it open and pour out the seed. Sow this immediately onto the surface of the 'mother' plant, where some mycorrhiza will be present in the compost.

The stem immediately behind the flower is swelling to form the seed capsule. Note how the spike has remained green up to this point, but has withered above.

The old flower remains at the end in a dried and shriveled state. At this stage, you can trim the petals back.

Watch for signs of splitting along these lengthwise ridges. Sow the seed fresh from the capsule.

1 *A developing seed capsule on Odontoglossum several weeks after pollination. Only the bottom flower on the spray was used. One capsule will provide more than enough seed.*

These are the remains of the column and the stigma, where the pollen was originally placed.

2 *Another capsule showing further development. The pear-shaped capsule is almost mature and will soon be ready for harvesting. Now is the time to prepare the 'mother' plant.*

3 *One seed capsule will produce a vast amount of seed. Use as much or as little as you like. Sprinkle it liberally all around the pot onto the surface of the compost.*

4 *If all goes well, you may expect to see results within a few months. The seed will form green protocorms from which leaves and roots will eventually grow.*

Sturdy seedlings after twelve months, now ready for individual pots.

Keep moist by submerging the plant in water to just below pot rim. Avoid washing the seed away.

Preparing orchids for a show

If you are interested in showing your orchids, start by entering the appropriate classes in your local flower show or joining an orchid group. They often have a table show at their meetings and most hold an annual show. The rewards are numerous; apart from the chance of winning a trophy, there is the opportunity of meeting other members with whom to discuss your plants. More experienced growers can enter national and international orchid shows, where competition for the highest awards is keen. Here we consider some of the points the judges look for.

Above: This Miltoniopsis *Rouge is at its peak for showing. All the flowers are fresh, with naturally arching spikes. No other training is needed. This superb plant is bound to catch the judge's eye.*

Raise these spikes slightly before the flowers open.

These flowers are drooping too low and need some support.

Wait until all the buds have opened before showing this plant.

Left: *This fine specimen plant of Miltoniopsis* Flamboyant *is of good show standard, but not yet ready and not well presented. A little attention now will produce good results later.*

Left: Unlabeled plants may be disqualified. Choose a small white or green card and clearly write or print the orchid name. Check with the show schedule that you have entered the right class.

COELOGYNE
OCHRACEA

This supporting cane can remain in place at the show.

Resurface with fresh compost if necessary, and wash the pot to make sure it is clean and presentable.

Right: A few simple precautions before traveling to shows will avoid damage to plants. Place your orchids in boxes to prevent them falling over and stake the ends of long flower spikes.

Insert a traveling cane to prevent damage during transit, but remove it at the show.

Above: Use soft plastic film or tissue paper to wrap around the flowers and protect them from damage while traveling. This is particularly useful when blooms overlap and might become bruised if crushed together.

Part Two

DISPLAYING ORCHIDS

Orchids have long been considered flowers of mystery and romance, an idea reinforced by legendary tales of their secret qualities passed down through countless generations and images of girls wearing orchids in their hair and orchid-filled garlands draped around their necks. The use of orchids as cut flowers is probably restricted to this century, and only in the last 20 years has their popularity seen such a massive increase that they have become readily available in our stores and garden centers. Even so, the number of orchid varieties grown commercially as cut flowers is small compared to the 25-30,000 species and many types or hybrids available throughout the world. Perhaps in years to come this number will continue to increase and many more varied and exciting varieties will be offered as cut flowers.

The lasting properties of orchids compares well with any other type of flower, even after being flown halfway around the world. In fact, even though most are nurtured in the carefully controlled conditions of a greenhouse, orchids will come to no harm in the home - provided they are carefully tended. Their striking color and unusual shapes certainly make them ideal subjects for flower arranging. This section of the book explores some of the ways in which you can use orchid flowers and plants to create beautiful displays. These range from wired corsages and handsprays for special occasions, to hand-tied bunches and everyday arrangements, some using cut flowers and some built up from living plants simply gathered together in their pots. Many different containers and accessories are featured in these displays, together with a varied selection of foliage material, all from common garden plants. We hope these ideas will inspire you to create interesting and exciting displays to brighten your home.

One of the many lovely hybrids of Miltoniopsis, *the popular pansy orchids.*

A bouquet of tumbling dendrobiums

You will need to master the basic skills of wiring and mounting flowers before tackling a project such as this, but the reward for a little extra care is a bouquet full of life and movement, created as much by the space around the flowers as by the component parts of the design itself. When viewing the bouquet from behind, the wires should resemble the spokes of a wheel, each one radiating neatly from the central securing point. Since these wires form the handle of the bouquet, reduce them to a length that allows the bouquet to balance easily in the hand without tilting forward. Tape the wires together with stem tape and finally, for appearance and handling comfort, bind the bouquet neatly and securely with a narrow satin ribbon.

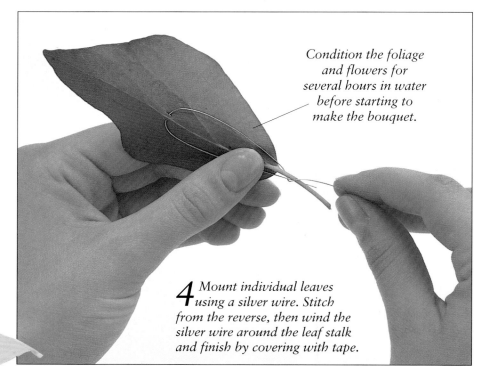

Condition the foliage and flowers for several hours in water before starting to make the bouquet.

4 *Mount individual leaves using a silver wire. Stitch from the reverse, then wind the silver wire around the leaf stalk and finish by covering with tape.*

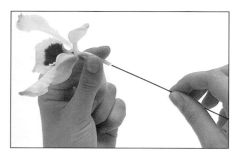

1 *Insert a wire through the stem into the back of the flower. The wire must be strong and springy, allowing the flower to 'bounce' without bending.*

2 *Pass a silver wire through the back of the flower, then wind it around the stem to hold it firmly in place. You will need a steady hand!*

To mount the flowers, use a very fine wire. Heavier flowers may require a thicker gauge wire.

3 *Cover the flower stalk and wire with a thin twist of stem tape, starting from the back of the flower head.*

5 *Secure and tape single flowers with the ivy leaves to form individual units. Take five units and arrange them into the basic design. Fix in position using silver wire to form a central securing point at the back of the bouquet.*

Soft green ferns contrast with the dark green of the ivy leaves.

You can substitute the individual flowers of Dendrobium Montrose AM/RHS used here with a range of other orchids in exciting shapes and colors.

Nephrolepis *fern*

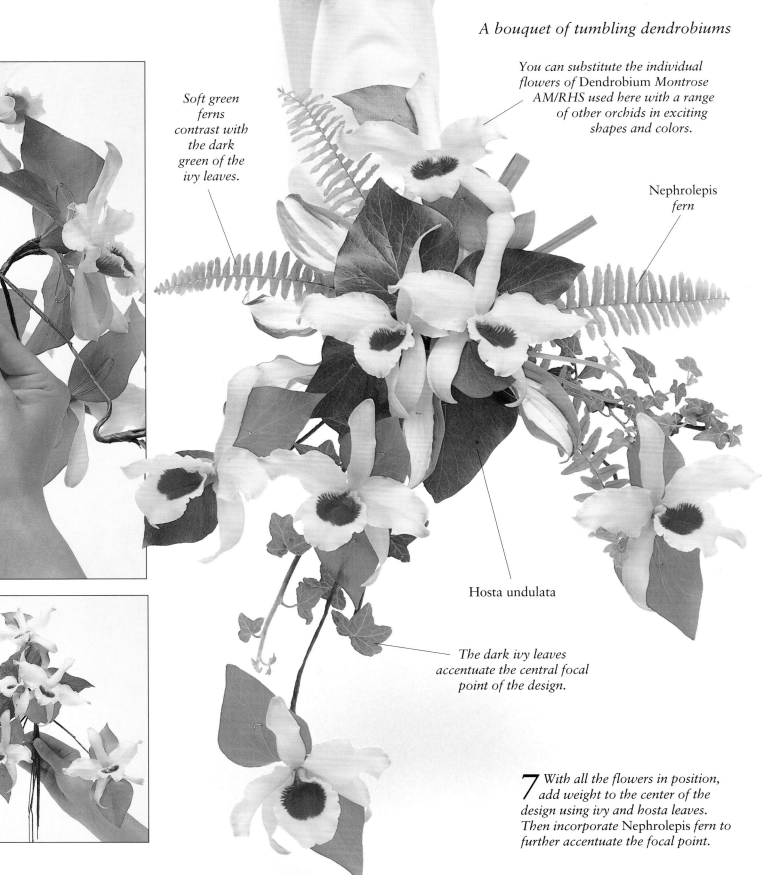

Hosta undulata

The dark ivy leaves accentuate the central focal point of the design.

6 *Taking the wires through the securing point, add two central flowers, placing them close together to form the focal point.*

7 *With all the flowers in position, add weight to the center of the design using ivy and hosta leaves. Then incorporate Nephrolepis fern to further accentuate the focal point.*

95

A crescent-shaped handspray

Using a foam bouquet holder to create this striking crescent-shaped handspray allows you to feature flowers and foliage on their own stems. This not only looks more natural, but means that once inserted into the wet foam, they last a long time. Naturally, the character of the design will depend on the type and color of the orchids you feature. Here, the choice of *Cochlioda noezliana*, with so many flowers elegantly displayed along their wiry stems, lends great movement to the design. The single flowers of *Epidendrum radicans* have been mounted on long thin wires to soften the whole appearance, while the more solid shape and severe lines of *Bifrenaria harrisoniae* form the focal point. These flowers also have the added bonus of being heavily scented. Do not be tempted to overcrowd the handspray with an excess of flowers; the impact of the design relies on the ability to see the form of the individual flowers. As you build up the design, be sure to take advantage of any natural curves, either on the stems of the orchids or the foliage, that will help to create and maintain the crescent shape. This colorful handspray would be perfectly suited as a presentation bouquet.

1 *Wet the foam bouquet holder, but do not oversoak it. Insert sprigs of foliage to outline the shape of the bouquet before adding any flowers. Allow the natural movement of the foliage to give a free-flowing look.*

Remove the leaves and side branches from the stems before inserting them into the foam.

The soft green foliage of juniper provides an excellent foundation for the handspray.

Cymbidium corsage

Cymbidiums are ideally suited to create this double corsage. Wire and tape the flowers and foliage, using the thinnest wire that will support each component part. Choose foliage to complement the colors of the orchids used.

Above: *Arrange the foliage around the flowers, uniting the wires to form a 'stem'.*

Right: *Cut to the required length and tape everything firmly.*

96

2 *Push the flower stems deeply into the wet foam of the holder so that they are held firmly. Add more foliage and continue to build the bouquet into the crescent-shaped design.*

The rich dark foliage gives depth and forms an integral part of the design.

3 *Develop a focal point by using more dominant flowers in the center. All the flowers and foliage must appear to spring from one point deep within the bouquet.*

The fiery orange-red flowers of Cochlioda noezliana.

The large fragrant flowers of Bifrenaria harrisoniae form the focal point of the bouquet.

Individually wired flowers of Epidendrum radicans provide a delicate, softening effect.

A hand-tied bouquet

This hand-tied bouquet is a simple gathering of flowers and foliage assembled in the hand. When choosing flowers and foliage to create a hand-tied bouquet, select stems of a good length, so that when the bouquet is complete you can cut the ends off level, and when placed in a vase, they will all be below the water level. First remove all flowers and leaves from the bottoms of the stems that would otherwise become damaged during the construction or tying. Condition both the flowers and foliage by standing the cut and trimmed stems in deep water for several hours. Finish off the completed bouquet with a large ribbon bow, making it perfectly suited as a presentation bouquet, being comfortable to hold or cradle across the arm. At the end of the evening you can simply drop the arrangement in a vase of water to create an instant display for a central point in the room.

1 *Select the tallest and straightest stems of flowers or foliage to form the central column around which to build the remaining material.*

Clean the ends of the stems of both flowers and foliage before starting to assemble the bouquet.

Graceful sprays of Oncidium Golden Shower dance like clouds of butterflies on wiry, branching sprays.

2 *Lay each stem at a slight angle to the original, turning the bunch slightly with each addition. Gradually build the stems into a spiral with the stems crossing at the same point.*

3 Mix foliage and flowers together as you build up the spiral. Finish off with some shorter stems of foliage to complete the shape.

4 Use a length of ribbon to hold the bouquet together. When complete, wind the ribbon around firmly and secure it without damaging the stems.

When you cut the stems off level, the bouquet will stand on a flat surface unsupported.

The vibrant red flowers of Renanthera *Anne Black* will last for several weeks in water.

The rich green leaves of Crocosmia *and* Polygonatum *add height, with hosta leaves around the base.*

5 Complete the bouquet by attaching a generous ribbon bow. Drop this lavish gathering of flowers and foliage into a suitable container for a spectacular but informal display.

Choose a deep, stable container to drop the flowers into.

Paphiopedilums - oriental style

Paphiopedilums have often been described as the most primitive of orchids and, with their long erect stems and single flowers, they make ideal subjects for an oriental-style arrangement. Here we have used a stoneware oven dish, but you could use any type of shallow container to hold this simple but stunning display. The straight lines and angular corners of the dish echo the simple lines of the bamboo, and the colors of both bamboo and dish complete the near perfect harmony of a display that uses just a few flowers. The display is arranged in two pin holders, both firmly secured into the dish with waterproof adhesive strips. In the wild, the stems of most paphiopedilums support their flowers high above the foliage. You can recreate this effect by positioning each flower so that its unusual and distinctive features can be clearly appreciated. The oriental flavor of the display has been emphasized by adding sprays of *Acer palmatum* around the base.

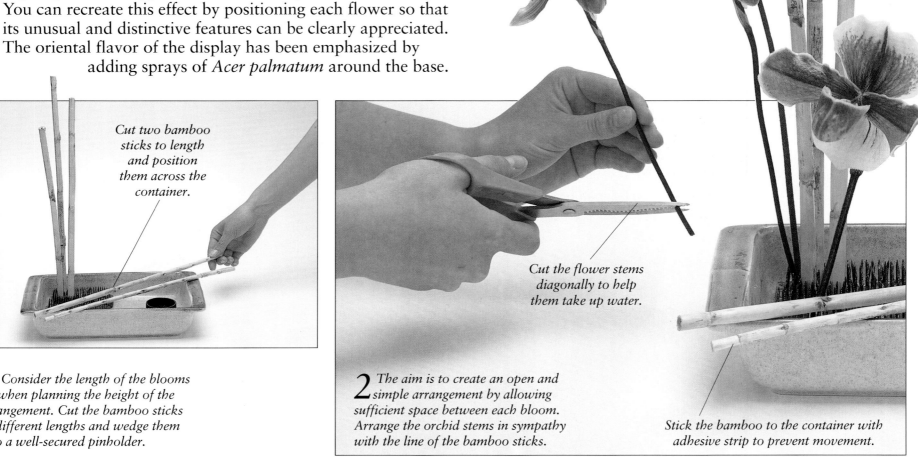

Paphiopedilum lawrenceanum

Paphiopedilum *Bar-maud*

Cut the flower stems diagonally to help them take up water.

Stick the bamboo to the container with adhesive strip to prevent movement.

Cut two bamboo sticks to length and position them across the container.

1 Consider the length of the blooms when planning the height of the arrangement. Cut the bamboo sticks to different lengths and wedge them into a well-secured pinholder.

2 The aim is to create an open and simple arrangement by allowing sufficient space between each bloom. Arrange the orchid stems in sympathy with the line of the bamboo sticks.

3 Insert short lengths of foliage into the base of the arrangement to add visual 'weight'. Cover the pinholder to complete the display.

4 Fill the dish with water so that the ends of the flowers and foliage are well covered. Notice how the rich green Acer foliage enhances the hint of green in the orchids' sepals and petals.

Paphiopedilum *Millionette x Wendbourne*

Paphiopedilum *barbatum*

5 To create extra interest, place more bamboo sticks in front of the arrangement to soften the lines of the base of the dish and extend the display out into the room.

101

Cool, green and classic

This arrangement is based on a low, classically decorated bowl with a lipped top that makes it ideal for use with wire mesh as a foundation to hold the flower stems because, once crumpled and fixed in place, the mesh will not move. Although wire mesh seems a little old-fashioned compared with foam, it does have the advantage of holding the stems completely immersed in water; foam tends to lose water relatively quickly and the bottom of the stems could become dry. To emphasize the soft green tones of the orchids, this display is built up around the stark, angular shapes of the unripe seedpods of the common peony-flowered garden poppy. Their dark blue-green color and rigid form act as the 'bones' around which the 'flesh' of the display is constructed. Shorter sprigs of foliage leaves around the base not only act as a foil to the flowers, but also hide the wire mesh from view. The subtle shades of lime green that dominate this display give it a gentle and soothing appeal that would suit both traditional and modern rooms.

3 Working from the center of the display outwards, insert short leaves and sprigs of foliage to cover the wire mesh in the base.

The unripe seedpods on the long, straight stems of the common peony-flowered garden poppy bring an unusual blue-green color to the display.

1 Crumple a piece of plastic-coated wire mesh and push it firmly into the bowl. This will anchor the stems and ensure that they are immersed in water.

Cut the stems cleanly and diagonally to help them take up water.

2 Cut the garden poppy stems to the required lengths and position them in the wire mesh base. Use these to outline the height, width and shape of the arrangement.

Wisteria leaves and the young shoots of heather provide a contrast in form but blend in with the color of the orchids.

Check that the water level covers all the stems and top up the bowl regularly to keep the display fresh.

4 Insert the longest-stemmed orchids carefully through the foliage and into the wire mesh. Select and locate these stems so that they are similar in height and width to the poppy heads already in position.

Use the natural curve of the stems to accentuate the design.

5 Add shorter-stemmed orchid flowers to the center front of the arrangement to develop a central focal point. Make sure that you insert these deep into the container so that they reach well below the water level.

The lime green flowers of Dendrobium Kasam Gold provide a stylish and understated appeal to this arrangement.

6 When you have placed the last of the orchids, complete the arrangement by filling in with foliage where you can see gaps. Remember to fill in the back as well as the front.

A mixed posy bowl

To make this small posy, you will need a bowl or dish that is deep enough to hold a generous reservoir of water in the base. Fix the foam securely into the container using either a foam anchor in the base of the bowl, or tape the block of foam firmly across the top using waterproof florist tape. This delightful little arrangement would be suitable either for a dining or an occasional table, as it can be viewed from all angles. It makes good use of a number of shorter-stemmed orchids in order to create an attractive arrangement whichever direction you look at it. The orchids featured here are in shades of yellows, golds, browns and greens that blend in with the soft tones of the *Nephrolepis* fern. Sprays of *Euonymus* and golden *Marjoram* foliage also add to the warm and pleasing appearance of the display.

Use a block of foam large enough to be raised well above the rim of the bowl.

1 *Secure well-soaked flower foam with florist tape, making sure that the end of the tape is fixed to the bowl. Pull the tape tightly over the foam to hold it firmly in the dish.*

2 *First create the overall shape of the design with ferns and other foliage. Turn the dish as you work so that you can view it from all sides.*

This stem of fern determines the finished height of the arrangement.

3 *Continue to build up the shape of the posy by adding more foliage. Finally, add the flowers, carefully pushing the stems into the wet foam.*

Paphiopedilum gratrixianum, *with its soft golden tones, stands proudly at the apex of the posy.*

5 When completed, this delightful mixed posy will continue to give you pleasure for a considerable time. If one of the orchids fades, simply replace it and in this way you will maintain the posy's fresh appearance.

The large-lipped, chestnut-spotted, yellow hybrid Odontocidium Tiger Hambühren.

Single stems of Lycaste Luciana *last well as a cut flower in this type of arrangement.*

4 Fill the container with water. To keep the flowers and foliage in good condition, spray them regularly with a fine mist sprayer. They will respond well to this type of treatment.

Odontoglossum *Rialto* x Odontioda *Pacific Gold*

The short stems of Dendrobium Montrose AM/RHS *are just long enough to be pushed into the foam.*

Cymbidium *Indian Tea, an early hybrid.*

Orchids with glass beads

Flower foam or chicken wire would be quite inappropriate materials for a modern arrangement in a square glass container such as this. Instead, glass beads have been chosen to hold the small number of flower stems firmly in position. Their soft green coloring plays an important part in creating a balance to the whole display. Place the glass beads into the container until it is approximately two-thirds full. If the orchids are tall and top heavy, you may need to add more beads to give the stems support. Several hours before starting the arrangement, condition the flowers and foliage by cutting the ends of the stems with a diagonal cut and standing them in deep water. Just two types of orchid make up this display. The rose-purple lip of the *Vanda tricolor* blends perfectly with the strong solid color of the *Masdevallia coccinea* to produce a stunning arrangement that is ideally suited to a modern setting. The central focal point has been created with just three *Hosta* leaves.

Glass beads are an alternative means of holding flower stems in position, particularly when just a few stems need supporting.

1 *Fill the vase until it is approximately two-thirds full of beads. Pour some water over the beads to moisten them and to make inserting the stems a smoother operation.*

2 *Push the flower stems as deep as possible into the beads to ensure that they are firmly gripped in place and well below the eventual water level.*

3 *Arrange three solid-green hosta leaves around the stems of the* Vanda tricolor *to create a focal point for this striking display.*

4 *Take care when pushing thin-stemmed flowers, such as this* Masdevallia, *into the glass beads. They are easily bent or broken.*

Vanda tricolor suavis *is a native of Java and was introduced into cultivation in 1846. It has heavily scented fleshy flowers.*

The most unusual waxy flowers of Masdevallia coccinea *sway on their wiry stems when exposed to the slightest movement of air.*

5 *Add water to just below the level of the glass beads. Do not be tempted to incorporate too many flowers or an excess of foliage, which will only spoil the dramatic effect created by the strong colors and simplicity of the display.*

A basket of dendrobiums

A small bowl filled with foam and securely anchored into this wide, flat basket with an arching, hooplike handle allows you to create a sumptuous arrangement, with the illusion of flowers piled up and spilling gracefully out over the sides of the basket. Basketware for flower arranging has become increasingly popular over the years and this display, being long and low and having an all-round appeal, would be perfect as the centerpiece for a dining table. By lifting it with one finger under the handle, you can easily and safely transfer it to an occasional or coffee table in another room. Before beginning any arrangement, carefully condition both flowers and foliage to extend their life as much as possible so that you can gain the best value from them. Cut the stems diagonally, exposing the maximum amount of cut area to the water. You may need to bruise the woody foliage stems with a hammer. Stand flowers and foliage in deep water in a cool place for several hours. Once this arrangement is complete, keep a careful eye on it; as the bowl in the basket is comparatively small and shallow, you must regularly top it up with fresh water.

3 Starting with the longest ones, insert the flower stems over the edge of the bowl, pushing them deep into the foam so that the flowers rest gently on the foliage.

As you reach the center of the basket, slightly increase the angle at which you push the flowers into the foam so that they become more vertical.

The handle should be strong enough to enable you to lift up the finished arrangement.

Press the container firmly onto two lengths of adhesive strip.

1 Cut a block of well-soaked foam to fit the container, but standing about 1in(2.5cm) above the rim. Secure the foam into the bowl with crossed lengths of florist tape.

2 Make use of the natural curves of the stems and allow the foliage to languish lazily over the bottom and sides of the basket.

Keep the handle of the basket a major feature of the design and do not completely obscure it with flowers.

Reviving wilted flowers

Flowers of the phalaenopsis type of dendrobium, imported in vast numbers from the Far East and used in this and several other displays in this book, may well arrive in a very soft, limp condition, particularly if they have traveled a long distance out of water. You can revive them perfectly by cutting about 0.5in(1.25cm) off the end of the stems and totally immersing the blooms in a bath of cold water. After about 30 minutes, the flowers become quite revived and are not damaged by the water. Stand them in deep water for several hours and condition as usual.

4 Continue building up the sides into a mound, keeping within the confines of the handle. Use the minimum amount of foliage, as the flowers should expand from deep inside the arrangement.

These pale green buds will open into the pure white flowers of the hybrid Dendrobium Big White.

Solid dark green leaves of Pulmonaria saccharata.

Dendrobium *Bom*

Paphiopedilums with shells

Placing shells in a clear glass bowl adds a considerable amount of interest to what is a very simple arrangement of just five flowers, all of the same species. The shells with their varied shapes, colors and textures not only add decorative interest within the bowl, but they also secure the foam in a central position and form a base for the arrangements. The foliage should not cover too much of the shells or the rim of the glass bowl. Arrange it carefully so that it seems to emerge from a central point within the bowl and, together with the orchids, appears to 'erupt' like a volcano. When complete, this charming arrangement shows off the paphiopedilums' dramatic shape to great effect. Often called the 'lady's slipper orchid', the paphiopedilums' subtle shades of color make them unique, even among other orchids. The flowers featured in this display are *Paphiopedilum barbatum*, a species from the Malay Peninsula and first introduced into cultivation in 1840.

Before inserting foliage into the foam, remove any side branches or leaves that would sit below the water level. This is a sprig of Buxus (box).

2 *Push individual leaves into the foam, taking care that they do not cover or spill over the rim of the bowl or hide the seashells from view.*

The thin, clear glass allows an uninterrupted view of the shells.

1 *Place a small block of wet foam in the center of the bowl and hold it firmly in place with an assortment of shells of various shapes and colors.*

5 Add water until the bowl is approximately two-thirds full. Top up the water level regularly and, given an occasional spray with a fine mist sprayer, the arrangement should last for two to three weeks.

3 Select each flower carefully, bearing in mind the angle from which it will be seen. Arrange some in profile to show off their unusual form.

4 Use the flowerheads of Alchemilla mollis to provide a contrasting texture. Foliage material is just as important as good-quality blooms.

To appreciate the subtle colors in this display, stand it against a plain background.

The species Paphiopedilum barbatum normally has one flower per stem, but occasionally two.

Add sufficient Alchemilla mollis to form a link between the individual leaves around the foam in the base of the container and the flowers and foliage above it.

1 *Cut a block of wet foam to size and secure it in the bowl. To do this, you can either use a foam anchor in the base of the bowl or secure the foam block across the top with florist adhesive tape.*

An extravaganza of phalaenopsis

A buffet table would be the perfect setting for this simple yet stunning arrangement in which the rich colors of the orchids are accentuated by the cool white china bowl that bears them. Although a considerable amount of foliage has been used in the early stages of preparation, it does not overpower the sprays of flowers. The silver-gray foliage of the *Pyrus* and sprays of young variegated ivy leaves contribute a lightness to the edges, while the darker foliage of the ferns and *Prunus* create a more solid central point from which the sprays of flowers emerge. More interest and height is added by the two stems of *Vuylstekeara* Cambria 'Plush' FCC/RHS rising out of the heart of the display, their wine-red petals and sepals contrasting with the warm pink of the phalaenopsis flowers. The silver-green seedheads of *Lunaria* (honesty) create further interest through the center of the display, completing the overall shape and blending perfectly with the other foliage used around the base. As an added bonus to their superb appearance, both phalaenopsis and vuylstekearas will last well as cut flowers.

2 *Push the stems of foliage well into the foam, allowing them to arch over the side of the bowl and establish the shape of the display. Add more foliage, working towards the center and keeping a low curved outline.*

Condition the foliage by cutting and standing it in deep water for several hours. Harder stems, such as Pyrus, *may need bruising with a hammer.*

Remove all the leaves from the ends of the foliage stems before inserting them into the foam.

3 Hold the stems of the phalaenopsis roughly in position before cutting them, so that when you push them into the foam they will arch over but not touch the table.

Cut the stems diagonally to give the maximum surface area in contact with the water.

4 Complete the arched effect by placing shorter stems towards the center. The wine-colored vuylstekearas bursting from the center make a dramatic impact.

Tall spikes of Vuylstekeara Cambria 'Plush' FCC/RHS.

Honesty seedheads

Phalaenopsis *Pink Chief x Zuma Cupid.*

These candy pink flowers of Phalaenopsis *Pink Chief x Fairvale* are perfectly spaced along the stem.

Handle the delicate phalaenopsis flowers with care, as they are easily bruised.

5 Sprays of Lunaria seedheads act as a foil to the tall vuylstekeara spikes. Fill in the area around the top of the bowl with foliage, taking care not to obscure the phalaenopsis.

113

Magenta magic

This sumptuous and boldly colored arrangement is based on a round china vase with a raised base that provides sufficient height for the flowers to flow down gracefully to the surface of the table. In addition, the bowl is generous enough to hold an ample amount of water and is the ideal shape to contain a mound of wire mesh to support the flower stems. At first sight, this display may seem extravagant in its use of flowers, but as an all-round arrangement destined to feature as the centerpiece on a large dining table, its striking appearance more than justifies its lavish use of ingredients. Do remember to keep the vase topped up with water, and an occasional spray with a fine mist sprayer will maintain the flowers at the peak of freshness. Before spraying, always move arrangements away from polished furniture to avoid marking the surface.

1 *Crumple the plastic-coated wire mesh into a ball the same size as the container, squeezing it into the bowl to create as tight a fit as possible.*

4 Continue building foliage in towards the center, leaving it quite open at this stage to allow easy access for the flower stems. Notice how the contrasting shapes of the foliage create an interest in their own right.

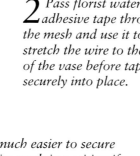

2 *Pass florist waterproof adhesive tape through the mesh and use it to stretch the wire to the edge of the vase before taping it securely into place.*

It is much easier to secure the wire mesh in position if you use a vase with a slightly lipped rim.

3 *Begin by placing foliage around the rim, carefully concealing any tape used to secure the wire. Turn the vase continually as you work to help you create a good balanced shape.*

Leave the stems of foliage long enough to penetrate deep into the vase.

A mound of wire is helpful when you insert stems that are to fall over the rim.

The small flower buds on the ends of these sprays of orchids are unlikely to open.

6 Space out the lacy flowerheads of Aegopodium, or ground elder, to resemble starbursts highlighted against a deep purple sky.

The deep magenta flowers of Dendrobium *Madame Pompadour.*

Foliage for impact

It is impossible to overemphasize the importance of foliage in flower arranging and in this book you can see how different types of foliage create different effects. It can form part of the display, act as a foil to the flowers, add weight to a display or make it light and airy, or simply serve to hide the mechanics of the support material. Whatever role it is to fill, choose it as carefully as you would the flowers, making sure it is clean and fresh. Cut the stems diagonally or, if they are hard and woody, bruise them with a hammer. Make sure they have a good long drink before using them in an arrangement.

5 Allow the natural curves of the flower stems to flow gracefully out from the sides of the display. Space the blooms sufficiently far apart so that you can see each one clearly in the final arrangement.

In contrast to the magenta flowers of the older hybrid Dendrobium *Madame Pompadour,* the more modern, larger flowers of Dendrobium *Sabeen* have a richer, warmer color and a velvety texture.

The large, white-edged leaves of Hosta decorata *and the mottled green of* Syngonium *provide a fitting background for this striking orchid arrangement.*

Sprigs of the small green leaves of common box and Euonymus *separate the stems of orchids and fill in the gaps.*

A living basket of orchids

Ficus benjamina

To many orchid lovers, cutting flowers to use them in an arrangement in the home would be quite alien. However, sharing their beauty as plants assembled into an attractive living display seems to make much more sense. The vibrant golden shades of this generously filled basket would lift the mood of any dark corner, or could be used to create a centerpiece for a dormant fireplace during the summer. With the exception of the *Masdevallia urosalpinx* peering over the rim of the basket, the orchids used in this display are all from the family Oncidiinae. The two taller orchids are excellent examples of training flower spikes with the minimum amount of support, allowing the stems to arch over and display their flowers to full advantage. Using a water-retentive aggregate in the bottom of the basket helps to increase the amount of moisture in the air around the plants and greatly reduce the risk of them suffering from the dry conditions usually found in the home. Keep this aggregate layer moist and spray the plants occasionally with a fine mist sprayer to maintain the display at a peak of freshness.

These expanded clay granules are ideal for creating a water-retaining layer in the base.

1 *Choose a deep wicker basket with an integral plastic lining and add sufficient moistened aggregate to form a humid 'microclimate' and raise the pots to a suitable level.*

2 *Settle the background foliage plant down firmly on the aggregate and position orchid plants with tall stems around it, working from the back of basket towards the front.*

3 *Before finally setting any plants into the display, it is a good idea to offer each one into its approximate position, then turn the plant first one way then the other to judge from which angle it looks best.*

The delicate flowers of Oncidium Gower Ramsey arch gracefully on springy stems.

A well-grown plant of Odonticidium Rupella, partially supported then allowed to arch over naturally.

6 *Use small ferns or moss to finish off the arrangement by covering the tops of the pots. The basket handle not only adds to the appearance of the display, but also makes it easy to move.*

4 *Avoid a top-heavy look by using some shorter orchids. These will need supporting to allow their flowers to peer over the rim of the basket.*

Rossioglossum williamsoni

The gaily colored Rossioglossum grande from Guatemala, affectionately known as the 'clown orchid' from the manlike structure in the center of the flower.

5 *An occasional light spray with a fine mist sprayer is very beneficial to the orchids in the dry conditions of the home. This will not harm the foliage plants used in this display.*

Masdevallia urosalpinx

A young plant of Odonticidium Tiger Hambühren.

Orchids with a twist

Using dried grasses, seedpods and cones to echo the natural colors of basketware containers creates a study in shapes and textures, accentuated by the natural ramblings of a twisted hazel branch. The subtle shades of the dried materials call for an orchid with colors that are not strident but which blend harmoniously with the dried elements, producing a simple but lovely design with enormous appeal. Sprays of the very long-lasting *Arachnis* Maggie 'Ouei', commonly known as the spider orchid, appear to be pushing their way out through the display, all springing from one point deep within the basket. Placing the arrangement on a shallow basketware tray adds considerably to the general proportions of the display as well as further reflecting the subtle shades of the orchids. Scattering a few cones on the tray, similar to those used in the arrangement, also helps to link all the elements together. The arachnis is an orchid most suited to being used as a cut flower and, providing you keep the container topped up with water, it will last for a very long time in perfect condition.

Twisted hazel, (Corylus avellana 'Contorta'), much loved by all flower arrangers for its striking appearance.

1 *Cut a block of well-soaked foam slightly oversize so that when you push it into the lined basket it is held tightly in position. Insert a branch of twisted hazel to form the central core of the arrangement.*

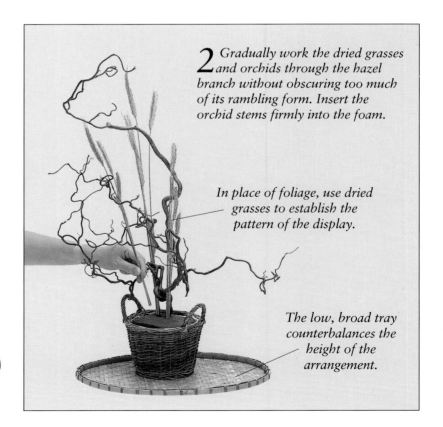

2 *Gradually work the dried grasses and orchids through the hazel branch without obscuring too much of its rambling form. Insert the orchid stems firmly into the foam.*

In place of foliage, use dried grasses to establish the pattern of the display.

The low, broad tray counterbalances the height of the arrangement.

118

3 Position the longest stems to flow over the edge of the basket and arch down almost to the table. Keep the stems sufficiently far apart so that you can appreciate the unusual shape of the flowers.

4 Use rich, dark brown fir cones, wired and taped in pairs, to fill in the center of the arrangement.

The unusual flowers of Arachnis Maggie 'Ouei' are perfect for this sculptural arrangement. The name is derived from the greek word 'arachne', meaning spider.

Dry options

The enormous diversity of basketware available today, in so many different shapes and sizes, and fashioned in materials from all over the world, gives great scope for flower arrangers to be experimental and inventive. Similarly, there is an ever-expanding range of dried materials, and many more we can gather from our own gardens. All these can be used so effectively with orchids to create displays that are both colorful and interesting.

5 Provide the final touch by placing a few fir cones on the tray, linking with those used in the main part of the arrangement. When the flowers have wilted, you can dismantle the display and save the dried material for future use.

Dried okra pods

An orchid-filled hamper

Many items around the home make suitable containers in which to build living displays of orchid plants. This wicker hamper is an excellent choice, being deep and square. Do make sure that it does not suffer from water damage by lining it with a double layer of plastic sheeting. Using a water-retentive aggregate in the bottom of the hamper will act as a safeguard against overwatering and help to produce a humid micro-climate more acceptable to the plants. The care taken to train, stake and tie the flower spikes as they grow will be rewarded when they come into bloom; staking the spikes very rigidly will produce a stiff, unnatural look, whereas insufficient tying will produce plants too ungainly to be used. The plants displayed here work together to provide a well-balanced and pleasing arrangement.

3 *Use bold foliage plants as a background to the orchids. This not only adds depth, but also improves the overall impact of the group.*

Ficus benjamina

1 *Select a container deep enough to allow the pots to sit inside and be hidden from view. Line it with a double thickness of plastic to form a waterproof tray.*

2 *Cover the base with a layer of aggregate to allow good drainage and also act as a moisture tray to maintain humidity.*

Secure the lid of the hamper in an open position before planting.

120

4 Select the position of each plant, with tall spikes at the center back and shorter arching ones to the front and sides.

5 Raise shallow pots by adding more stones to bring their flowers up into the required position or stand them on upturned pots or blocks of wood .

Vuylstekeara
Cambria 'Plush'
AM/RHS

6 Conceal the pots from view by dropping in small ferns or other foliage plants. Alternatively, placing decorative moss will have the same effect of finishing off the group.

Odontioda
cooksonii x
Wilsonara
Lyoth Ruby

Dancing flowers of
the pansy orchid
Miltonia *Limelight.*

Masdevallia
coccinea x
trochilus

Masdevallia
infracta

Small Nephrolepis
ferns dropped in to
conceal the pots.

Oncidium
Puch

121

Index to Orchids

***Right:** A striking* Oncidium *hybrid.*

Credits

The majority of the photographs featured in this book have been taken by Neil Sutherland and are © Colour Library Books. The publishers wish to thank the following photographers for providing additional photographs, credited here by page number and position on the page (BL: Bottom left, TR: Top right).

Eric Crichton: 36(BL), 37(TR), 38(TR), 39

Daan Smit: 82(TR)

Acknowledgements

The publishers wish to thank Brian Rittershausen and the staff of Burnham Nurseries in Newton Abbott, Devon for their generous help and patience while providing facilities for location photography. The majority of the plants featured in the first part of the book are from Burnham Nurseries. Thanks are also due to Ena and Joe Haywood for providing superb windowsill and conservatory locations. Gill and David Oakey would like to thank Pepi Dilullo and Lawrence Hobbs for providing plant material for some of the photographs featured in the second part of the book.